Reminiscences of an American Composer and Pianist

George Walker

The Scarecrow Press, Inc.
Lanham, Maryland · Toronto · Plymouth, UK
2009

SCARECROW PRESS, INC.

Published in the United States of America
by Scarecrow Press, Inc.
A wholly owned subsidiary of
The Rowman & Littlefield Publishing Group, Inc.
4501 Forbes Boulevard, Suite 200, Lanham, Maryland 20706
www.scarecrowpress.com

Estover Road
Plymouth PL6 7PY
United Kingdom

British Library Cataloguing in Publication Information Available

Library of Congress Cataloging-in-Publication Data

Walker, George, 1922–
  Reminiscences of an American composer and pianist / George Walker.
    p. cm.
  Includes bibliographical references and index.
  ISBN 978-0-8108-6940-0 (hardback : alk. paper) — ISBN 978-0-8108-6941-7
(ebook)
  1. Walker, George, 1922– 2. Composers—United States—Biography. 3.
Pianists—United States—Biography. I. Title.
  ML410.W278A3 2009
  780.92—dc22
  [B]
                                2009008547

In memory of Dr. George T. Walker
and Rosa K. Walker

I cannot always stand upon the peak and touch the stars.
Sometimes the wind is thick with snow and bleak,
And there are scars of sorrows that are long since past.

—from Stars by Susan D. Keeney

Contents

Preface

$\mathcal{T}$he first serious consideration that I gave to writing an autobiography occurred after I was asked to lecture to a special class at Rutgers University in Newark, New Jersey, in the spring of 1992. The director of the Honors Program had requested that I discuss my experiences in music with all of the students in this program a few weeks prior to my retirement, a mandatory decision forced upon tenured faculty by Rutgers University when they reach the age of seventy.

After the conclusion of the lecture, several students found my recollections intriguing. The director, who was present, suggested that I write a book about my life. When she affirmed that the Rutgers University Press would have an interest in publishing my memoirs, I contacted their office. I was told that they did not publish autobiographies.

After leaving Rutgers University, I resolved to devote all of my energy to composing and to recording. In June of 2008 I began, while working on *Da Camera*, a chamber orchestra score, to make notes of impressions and events that kept recurring to me. By November of 2008 I had written about thirty pages, adding material to an opening paragraph that would lead to the final paragraphs that I had written.

I continued to spend more time in jotting down memories of events relating to the development of my career as a pianist first, and then as a composer. This led me to contemplate the possibility of finding a company that would be interested in publishing my autobiography. I decided to approach the Scarecrow Press after recalling that in 1978 they had published an important interview of me in a discourse entitled *The Black Composer Speaks*.

When I spoke with Stephen Ryan, the senior arts and literature editor of Scarecrow Press, to discuss the project, I was delighted to have a positive response from him. He put me in touch with Blair Andrews, his assistant, and William Banfield.

When it became necessary for me to retrieve some documents from the Woodruff Library of Emory University, which houses my archives, Kathleen Shoemaker and Theresa Burk were very helpful in providing the requested material. When I disclosed that the book that I had begun was nearly completed, my sons, Gregory and Ian, both gifted writers, were pleased to learn that I was following in their footsteps.

Early Years

My mother, Rosa King Walker, remarked on more than one occasion that summer vacations for children were too long. Summers in Washington, DC, were always hot and very humid. Temperatures hovered around ninety degrees every day.

When my mother heard that Miss Mary L. Henry, a piano teacher who lived in southwest Washington, taught children in our neighborhood, she arranged for me to take piano lessons from her. I was five years old on June 27, 1927. My sister, Frances, who was two and a half years younger than I, began her piano lessons when she was four and a half years old.

Miss Henry was a tiny lady with a slightly raspy voice. Her eyes seem to twinkle when she smiled. When she was somewhat satisfied with my grasp of the pieces on the pages that she had assigned for my lesson, she rewarded me by placing a gold star on the first of those pages. Miss Henry would have little piano recitals periodically for her students. Our home became the site for these programs.

We had an upright piano in our parlor. During these modest recitals, my mother would observe the program while crouched on the steps of the staircase leading to the second floor of our home. With the drapes drawn back in the parlor she had a bird's-eye view of the proceedings taking place on the first floor. Neither my mother nor my father had any musical training. My mother had a light soprano voice. She could read music, but I never heard her touch the piano. Once she recalled a compliment that the music teacher in her high school paid her. The teacher told my mother that "she could listen to her sing all day." My father could neither read music nor play the piano. Sometimes on a Sunday evening he would attempt to pick out the melody of a hymn. The silence between notes was deafening.

My father, Artmelle George Theophilus Walker, emigrated to this country from Kingston, Jamaica. He was the oldest of several children. His father died when he was quite young. Intent upon providing some income for his family, my father became apprenticed to a tailor without any previous experience. After observing the sewing and stitching of an employee through the window of the shop, he applied for and received a job.

When he decided to improve his financial situation, my father left Jamaica with thirty-five dollars in his pocket on a boat that was destined for the United States. It was tossed perilously on the ocean during a violent storm. One Sunday evening when I was just a youngster, he graphically described the chaos of dishes being smashed and tables upturned in the dining room of the vessel.

He had no contacts in this country, no friends or relatives. The menial jobs that he accepted for survival—selling newspapers and stoking furnaces—left him dissatisfied. The idea of returning to school occurred to him in an epiphany when his employer asked him what he planned to do after leaving his only source of income. When my father stated, without prior consideration of an objective, that he wanted to further his education, his employer offered him a job in the summer after the end of an academic year.

My father enrolled in the medical school of Howard University in Washington, DC. He was a brilliant student. But an experience with a professor on the medical faculty predicated his decision to transfer to the medical school of Temple University, from which he graduated in 1918. He was one of four black students in his class. His first year of general practice was in Springfield, Massachusetts. This was the year of the influenza pandemic that killed many more persons than soldiers who died in combat in World War I. Twenty-eight percent of Americans were affected by the flu.

He returned to Washington, DC, after one year in Springfield. The winter had been too severe for him in Massachusetts. My father became the first physician to settle in an underdeveloped section of northwest Washington, DC. His medical practice flourished. Acquiring several homes within a few blocks of our house, he was the most respected person in that area.

Dr. George T. Walker

My father was a small man. His composure belied an attentiveness and concentration wherever he was. His silence in a room created an aura of Olympian authority. He seldom initiated a conversation when he was at home, preferring instead to listen to our conversation with critical ears. When he made a comment, his speech was clear, precise, and laconic—a clipped, slightly British articulation without the inflected syllables of many West Indians. It was never prefaced by "well," "ahs," or "ums."

His sense of humor, which he contained while in the midst of his family, endeared him to his patients and friends. His dedication to helping others was a calling with a deep religious significance. Linked to his accomplishment as a self-made man was a pride in having found the path from which he was never deterred. Beneath the reserve that was a large part of his demeanor was an extraordinary intensity of will and conviction that could explode with passion.

My father became the cofounder of two black medical clubs. (The American Medical Association did not permit black physicians to become members of its society.) They were comprised mostly of West Indian physicians, some of whom were graduates of the Howard University Medical School, who practiced medicine in Washington, DC. At each meeting a physician would present a paper on a topic of his choice. When it was my father's turn, one sensed that his preparation induced a degree of excitement in him as he anticipated the event.

The residents of this section of the city were predominantly black citizens. There were a few small grocery stores owned by Jewish families whose contacts within the neighborhood did not extend beyond their storefronts. And there were chain grocery stores, an A&P and Safeway, staffed entirely by white employees. There was one barber shop in the neighborhood. My father, with his own electric clippers and scissors, took pains to cut my hair when he determined that it was getting too long.

The exterior of our home differed from that of the other five red-brick houses on the block of 3200 Sherman Avenue, Northwest. My father's office was in the basement. Patients entered into it by descending two steps to the door below. The steps had been constructed by reducing the size of the front lawn plot.

Sherman Avenue was a tree-lined street where oaks dumped hundreds of acorns on sidewalks and curb areas in the fall. City officials expanded the road to accommodate express buses, which were filled with white persons headed from the outer limits of the city to the central business district in downtown Washington, DC, without making a single stop.

Directly across from our home was one of four houses that my father owned in the city. The occupants were two unmarried ladies, Miss Betty and Miss Maggie, who were seldom seen. The only brief conversation with them that I can recall happened when my father asked me to collect the rent money from them.

My father enjoyed the challenge of a job requiring manual effort. I can still visualize him from our front steps, a shadowy form atop their roof, patching a leak with a bucket of tar beside him.

Two doors down from our home was another house that my father owned, and three blocks south on the corner of Irving Street was the third house. In another section of the city, at 1956 Second Street, was the fourth house. It had two flats.

When my father decided to replace the flooring in our house, he engaged a carpenter to install the hardwood. At the end of the first day, after closely observing the worker, he called the worker's employer to cancel the appointment for the following day. My father learned enough by observing the carpenter to finish the job himself. It would be impossible to detect where the worker had stopped and where my father resumed the flooring. Waxing the varnish that he applied caused us untold grief. Every two years my mother and I would spend hours on sore, aching knees removing the dirty wax coating with steel wool. My father applied another layer of varnish after we finished.

Our backyard was not an area for socializing. My father had a predilection for fresh eggs, which he ate sunny-side up every morning for breakfast. A small chicken shack housed several birds. A rooster announced the break of day, defying any city code that might have existed then. A large bathtub swarmed with huge goldfish that survived layers of ice in the winter. A small garden produced beautiful eggplants. Grapevines suspended on a sturdy trellis attracted a stream of intimidating bees that surrounded the succulent, dark bluish fruit of Concord grapes. The narrow sidewalk paralleling the neighbor's fence led past a window that was opened only when wheelbarrows of coal from a fuel company were shoveled directly into the basement floor, filling it almost to the ceiling. Part of the basement, separated from my father's office, was occupied by two washtubs on one wall and the furnace near the other wall. The remaining space was a small central area where my father hatched baby chicks, cured ham, and made delicious root beer.

The country place that my father purchased was not a cultivated plot of land. A tenant lived in the house above the sloping acres where wild raspberries and strawberry vines could entangle the feet. Junk, consisting of auto parts on the property, was never removed. Before the house could be reached from the dirt road off of the main highway, there were bountiful peach trees and a few tall pear trees bearing fruit that was inaccessible without climbing them.

My mother, Rosa King, obtained a job in the Government Printing Office in Washington, DC, after graduating from M Street High School (later Dunbar High School) when she was sixteen. She was able to support my grandmother, a single parent whose second husband died when my mother was a young child. My grandmother's first husband was sold at a slave auction and was never seen again. She fled north with friends in the middle of the night from a plantation in Virginia. When they approached Washington, DC, they encountered the Union Army and freedom. They had successfully escaped the despicable tyranny and inhumanity of the Confederacy. When I ventured to ask my grandmother what it was like to be a slave, she replied, "They did everything except eat us."

My mother's gifts were apparent to all who knew her. Her mind was remarkably agile. Her speech, flawless (without any regional accent) and quick to respond, dominated every conversation. Slang, even the ubiquitous "okay," was never used by either parent. She had a very special talent for arithmetic, and she was a superb bridge player. The unassuming bond between her and my grandmother was remarkable.

There was an unusual, innate directness about my mother that was evident in her gaze and her ability to convey an opinion that was not coated with malice or envy. She enjoyed laughing about the foibles of others while understanding the fragility of their situation. She was a magnet to which persons with problems gravitated because they sensed her empathy. She also had psychic powers. Foreseeing in a dream the closing of banks by Franklin D. Roosevelt in his first days in office in 1933, she withdrew our savings the next day. When her health deteriorated in Washington, DC, before my sister became her caretaker in New York, two neighbors—Mrs. Smith, who lived next door, and Mrs.

Rosa King Walker, circa 1918

Valencia, who lived several houses down from us on the same block—
would come directly from their jobs in the late afternoon to sit and talk
with my mother for an hour before going to their homes.

My mother fervently believed in the importance of education. In the
summer she organized class sessions in math and English for the children
on our block. Out of her personal expense budget she paid for the college
education of one of my cousins, Natalie Robinson. Her brother, Thorn-
ton, was my favorite cousin. (One afternoon he brought us the most delicious vanilla ice cream from a local creamery that I have ever tasted.)

When my mother learned from my father that a talented piano
student, Robert Nolan, a complete stranger, could not complete his
senior year at Howard University because he was virtually penniless, she
and my father not only paid his tuition but also provided clothes and
meals for him. After his graduation from Howard University, Nolan
had to be reminded by his piano teacher, Cecil Cohen, that he had not
expressed his gratitude for the support that my parents had given him.
Nolan went to Detroit where he established the Robert Nolan School
of Music. He adopted the title of "Dean," a designation that obsessed
him as an undergraduate music major at Howard University.

In our household there were never arguments about anything. It
was difficult for me to realize later in life that this was an anomaly. We
as a family were atypical in so many ways. We lived in the present, not
in the past. The daily routine that controlled our existence made each
special event more pleasurable. My parents had no desire to inflate their
standing in the community. They never considered moving out of the
area. Their generosity reflected a constant awareness of their good fortune. Hard work, frugality, humility, and an unstained character were
among the ultimate virtues that my mother constantly espoused. She
was the spokesperson for my father.

My uncle, John King, who was my mother's brother, lived with us.
His room was one of two added to our house by my father. It was connected to my tiny room on the second floor by a door. My uncle worked
as a butler during World War I for Robert Lansing, the secretary of
state under President Woodrow Wilson. The telegram announcing the
end of the war was first received by my uncle, whose photo appeared in
newspapers all over the country.

Children amused my uncle. When he took another job at the
Wardman Park Hotel in Washington, DC, he would come home in

the evening with a bag of food to cook for his dinner and cream si-
phoned into a pint flask of Seagram Whiskey. A touch of this mixture,
combined with sugar and a small can of Campbell's beans, can be ad-
dictive.

My sister and I would impatiently await his arrival to pester him
for boxes of Hershey Bars that he sometimes brought us. My mother
would vainly attempt to hide them beyond our reach. But she didn't
reckon with our persistence in searching for the candy. By standing on
a chair, we found that the top of the china closet became accessible.

When I left for college, my cousin, Gladys Jackson, who was born
in Virginia, came to live with us. Thanksgiving and Christmas were
joyous holidays when all of our closely related cousins gathered in the
small spaces of our home for a festive turkey dinner. My mother loved
company and my father was a genial host as he brandished the sharpened butcher knife before the dismemberment of the bird began.

Our house was always abuzz with activity, conversation, and telephone calls for my father. With three phones in the house, it was impossible to determine beforehand if the calls were personal or business
related. I assumed the responsibility of responding to the first rings.
Friends and relatives dropped in unexpectedly to our delight. All chores
ceased while my mother chatted with them. These interruptions posed
no problem for my piano practice as I was not committed to it until my
matriculation at Oberlin College in 1937.

My grandmother, Malvina King, was the quiet presence, the only
generational link that connected my sister, Frances, and myself in our
childhood and adolescence with a bygone period. She could neither
read nor write. She was well into her eighties when I was in high school,
though we never knew exactly what her age was. No breakfast at 7:30
a.m. was finished before my grandmother had seated herself across
from us at the dining room table. She had lost all of her hair except for
several pure white silken strands that crisscrossed the top of her head.
She spent the entire day helping my mother in the kitchen—washing
dishes, preparing vegetables, ironing laundry, or canning fruit from my
father's country place. Extraordinarily gentle, with a shyness that made
eye contact impossible for her if strangers were present, she was my
mother's constant companion in the house. My mother disliked nick-
names. But for my grandmother I was "T," my middle initial. My father
always called me "George T."

A DEFINING EXPERIENCE

In the summer when my sister, Frances, was five years old, my parents drove to Northumberland County in Virginia to visit three families related to my mother as cousins. My grandmother remained at home. This was my second visit to the area.

There was a sequence that my mother adhered to. First, we spent three nights with Cousin Mary, two nights with Cousin Lila, and then made the brief trip to Reedville on the Chesapeake Bay, where fishing and crabbing were the major industries, to lodge with Cousin Margaret.

The pleasantness of the afternoon at Cousin Mary's was shattered when a young girl, an older cousin, with whom my sister had been playing burst into the porch area with the electrifying report that my sister was engulfed in flames. They had been playing with matches in the attic of the house. My mother rushed upstairs to beat out the flames. The burns on the right side of my sister were very severe. The next morning we left Cousin Mary's house at 4:00 a.m. in my father's small Buick to return to Washington, DC. My mother, in the backseat, cradled my sister wrapped in blankets for the entire journey home. I sat with my father in the front passenger seat without ever dozing off for the entire six-hour trip. The text of Schubert's "Erlkönig" would be an appropriate description of this harrowing life-threatening experience. My father rewrote the ending of the poem. My sister survived.

Her long and painful recovery was made possible by the attentive and imaginative treatment administered by my father and a wonderful black surgeon. Dr. Carson performed two remarkable skin transplants for my sister's right arm in his private hospital. The anguish that my parents must have experienced from this ordeal and years of constant treatment was never voiced. They were sustained by faith and accepted this misfortune without recrimination.

NEIGHBORS AND FRIENDS

I learned to read easily when I was quite young. My mother, who always put my sister and me to bed at 8:00 p.m., was unaware that I would surreptitiously turn on the light above my bed to read after she left us. This may have contributed to the myopia that required me to wear eyeglasses when

I was nine years old. Early to bed, early to rise was a motto of my mother. She would awaken me at 6:00 a.m. every morning (weekends included) without ever using an alarm clock to arouse me from my slumber.

The books that I read fueled my imagination, and I enacted the stories in games that I would create with the two boys who lived next door. The Smith family consisted of five children and four adults. They became impoverished after the tragic death of the children's father, who fell off a scaffold. My mother became one of their principal benefactors. Leona, the youngest of the children, became a close companion for my sister during her illness. The boys, Kessler and Henry (Bubba), who were older than I, were always available in the summer to play games with me—marbles, cards, horseshoes, baseball, football, sprinting down the street, fashioning bows and arrows in their yard, playing in the alley behind my father's garage or on the empty lot on the corner of Sherman Avenue and Kenyon Street. I loved to organize baseball and football games with my friends in the neighborhood.

The segregated elementary school that we attended, B. K. Bruce Elementary School, was a block away from our homes. It had an unattractive playground covered with gravel. Monkey bars suspended over the concrete pavement were the only playthings in the yard. I overcame the fear of falling to the ground by testing my stamina on them when no one else was around.

The school was perched above a mound of dirt two stories high from the main entrance on Sherman Avenue. In the early spring the hill would be covered with dandelions. After numerous entreaties from my grandmother, I climbed the slope to fill a bucket of weeds to satisfy her penchant to make dandelion wine. But I had no interest in tasting it when she had finished the brew. She could not complain about it being "adulterated," a term she regularly applied to products that she disdained.

ELEMENTARY AND JUNIOR HIGH SCHOOL

When I was enrolled in the fourth grade at B. K. Bruce Elementary School, one of the teachers, who was also the daughter of one of my father's patients, would confide in my mother about her personal problems. My father had successfully diagnosed her mother's cancer in sufficient time to control the disease. In one of the conversations that Rosa

DeSouza had with my mother, Rosa suggested that I take an IQ test. I remember becoming bored by page after page of simple questions in the exam. Despite my increasing lack of concern for providing the correct answers, the result of the exam was sufficiently impressive. I was permitted to skip two entire grades by going to summer school for two summers.

The summer school that I attended was in another section of Washington, DC. I don't even remember its name. My father drove me to and from the school. Hot, sticky air permeated the classroom. All of the windows were open; large black flies were everywhere. Most of the students there were repeating a grade that they had failed. I learned virtually nothing except some basic algebra. After these classes were completed, I was able to begin the seventh grade.

Garnet-Patterson was the closest junior high school to my home. It was slightly more than a mile away. Every day several friends from my neighborhood would ring our doorbell at 8:15 in the morning. Together we would walk rather briskly to the school in order to arrive in our classrooms before the bell sounded at 9:00 a.m. Boys and girls were in separate homerooms. After the placid atmosphere of B. K. Bruce Elementary School, Garnet-Patterson Junior High School seemed to be wildly out of control. Lack of discipline was in evidence, from the principal, the teachers, and the boys who came from other sections of the city. Although there was no real rowdiness by today's standards, there was always an underlying tension created by kids from different backgrounds.

There was a small grocery store directly across from the main entrance of the junior high school. At 12 noon, lunchtime, the boys in my classroom would be lined up in the hallway outside of the classroom. When the bell rang to signal the lunch break, the entire line of boys would stream pell-mell down the stairs, crossing the street to pour into the store. Clutching my lunch box, I found it impossible to break free of this human torrent until it had reached the street. Peeking inside the store, I was amazed to see how many boys could hardly wait to get a particular pickle out of the salty, foamed brine of a pickle barrel.

S. G. Fletcher was my homeroom teacher at Garnet-Patterson Junior High School. Maurice, one of the boys in our room and a favorite of the teacher, had become the editor for the school newspaper. Fletcher asked me to assist him in choosing submissions for publication. I found the task of selecting poems and articles interesting. But the most exciting event of those three years occurred in the gym.

Hudson, one of my friends who accompanied me to school in the morning, told me about the basketball team. I showed up once or twice in the gym for practice. Several weeks later, Hudson informed me that the team's last game would decide the city championship. I sat on the bench with him during the course of the game. We exhorted the coach to put us in as substitutes. The coach, maintaining a calm mien, ignored our frantic pleas as the closing minutes approached. The opposing team led by a point. The best player on our squad was "Mice" Anderson. With seconds remaining, he retrieved a ball and shot. To our great astonishment a swish followed the descent of the ball through the hoop. We had won the game without participating in it. Pandemonium ensued as we rushed onto the court to embrace Mice. The exuberance of victory is impossible to describe.

The progress that I was making in my piano lessons from Miss Henry became so rapid that it became clear to her and to my parents that I had surpassed her capacity to teach me. This dilemma became even more significant after a rather unusual occurrence. A white woman was walking past our house when she heard the sound of my piano. She rang the doorbell and asked who was playing. When my mother informed her that I was making the music, she excitedly repeated, "I've got to have him." The realization that others could recognize my talent added to my mother's confusion about a choice of another piano teacher.

JUNIOR DEPARTMENT OF MUSIC, HOWARD UNIVERSITY

When my mother heard about the Junior Department of Music at Howard University, she was not initially convinced that enrolling me in their program was the right step. But no one could suggest an alternative. We had no connections with any knowledgeable person who could recommend a private piano instructor in Washington, DC. When my mother applied for my admission into the Junior Department, I was assigned to Mrs. Lillian Mitchell. Only classical music was studied in this preparatory school. Jazz was for dancing and the uncultured rung of black society in Washington, DC.

Mrs. Mitchell was one of two teachers in a program that was supervised by Miss Camille Nickerson. Miss Nickerson, born into New Orleans, had been trained as a pianist. After graduating from the Oberlin Conservatory of Music, she began to give recitals that reflected her Creole background. She arranged concerts in which she appeared in native dress. These programs included her arrangements of some Creole melodies.

In addition to teaching in the Junior Department, Mrs. Mitchell also taught music education in the college music department at Howard University. She obtained her doctorate in music education during the years in which I studied piano with her and was the only person in the music department with that degree. She was, to the best of our knowledge, the only black person with a doctorate in music anywhere.

Each piano student in the Junior Department of Music received two half-hour lessons a week. The more advanced students also met for an hour on Saturday. A class conducted by Miss Nickerson was held in the basement of a two-story wooden structure. A grassy plot separated this building thirty yards from the even more decrepit music building of Howard University. The facilities inside the college structure were poor. The buildings appeared to have been homes originally, with little exterior or interior distinction. The first floor of the Junior Department building had two adjacent teaching studios separated by a panel that could be parted. Miner Teachers College was located in a fenced area about ten yards north of the music department's building.

I had good reasons for disliking the Saturday class. When I joined the Howard Cubs, a boys organization that met twice a week in the gym of Howard University, I was only able to participate in the basketball and swimming activities for less than an hour on Saturdays. Before I could leave in the morning to go to the university, I had weekly chores to do at home. By the time that I arrived at the gym at 10:00 a.m. and changed clothes, there was little playtime before I had to scoot across the campus to listen begrudgingly to a talk about musical subjects at 11:00 a.m. I was uncomfortable in being the youngest person there and often being only one of two boys present in a group of older, attractive girls. Years later I realized the importance of the effort that Miss Nickerson had made in recounting in this class the contributions of black concert artists (all singers) whose careers began in Europe.

My piano lessons with Mrs. Mitchell were primarily devoted to playing the correct notes and rhythms of a composition. One particular lesson in which she tried to explain how to fit two notes against three remains etched in my mind. I don't remember playing a piece from beginning to end for her. The music that she assigned to me was often more advanced than I was. Given a choice of learning the Brahms Rhapsody in B Minor and the Chopin Barcarolle, I wisely opted for the Brahms.

For four years, I would be excused from the last period of the school day at Garnet-Patterson Junior High School and Dunbar High School to meet my father, who would be waiting in his car to drive me to Howard University. He was never late. I have never known anyone who was as punctual as he was. After my piano lesson, he would take me home without saying a word. My mother would have dinner ready for us after we arrived.

Raymond, one of my two best friends in junior high school, took violin lessons in the Junior Department at Howard University from Louia Vaughn Jones. Mr. Jones had the distinction of playing a violin concerto with the National Symphony. But he never played in public when I was a preparatory student. Whatever career that he might have had was certainly behind him.

When I would visit Raymond on a Saturday afternoon, I would sometimes play the accompaniment for the Dvorak Humoresque and other works with him. (He had to restrain his ebullient English bulldog first.) But my principal delight in being in his spacious home was in having the opportunity to play table tennis on his pool table.

My other friend, Townsend, had taken piano lessons briefly. But I never heard him play. Each time that I would visit him, he would find the music for Paderewski's Minuet in G, Rachmaninoff's C-sharp Minor Prelude, Beethoven's Moonlight Sonata, and "Clair de Lune" by Debussy and insist that his mother, a sweet-tempered lady, come to the piano to listen to my playing of these works. She was unduly awed. I would be invited to stay for a beautifully prepared dinner with his rather morose father at the head of the table.

HIGH SCHOOL

Upon graduating from junior high school, I enrolled in Dunbar High School. Black students in segregated Washington, DC, were given a choice of attending one of three high schools. Dunbar High School, named after the poet Paul Laurence Dunbar, had an academic curriculum. Students who attended Dunbar were expected to go to college. Armstrong High School and Cardozo High School provided vocational training. Although Dunbar High School was located across the street from Armstrong High School there was no intermingling of students with entirely different perspectives and goals. Edward Kennedy "Duke" Ellington attended Armstrong High School, which he left three months before his graduation in 1916.

Dunbar was clearly elitist. It was considered to be the best black high school in the country. Its graduates included the distinguished physician and research scientist Charles Drew, who contributed significantly to the use of blood banks for American and British soldiers in World War II. I remember quite vividly watching my father enter the room that we called the library and telling my mother, who was in the kitchen, that Dr. Drew had been killed in an automobile accident. Drew had been on the faculty of the medical school at Howard University.

Edward Brooke, the first black senator elected to Congress by popular vote, graduated from Dunbar High School a year ahead of me. As a boy, he attended St. Luke's Episcopal Church where he became the crucifer. My friend, Townsend, who was an acolyte in this church, could hardly wait to succeed him in that position. Eddie Brooke was the first senator to demand the resignation of President Nixon. Campaigning in Massachusetts for a Senate seat, he intentionally denied the existence of de facto segregation in Boston in order to obtain support from white voters for his bid. His career in the Senate, however, was marked by his support for affirmative action, nondiscriminatory housing opportunities, and the extension of the 1965 Voting Rights Act. After leaving the Senate, a scandalous affair with well-spotlighted TV anchor, Barbara Walters, was disclosed.

Despite its reputation, Dunbar High School, which was presumed to have a highly qualified staff and a faculty at that time with master's degrees (not PhDs as some have reported), was a mixed bag. There were a few fine teachers with high standards and others who simply showed up to get their paycheck. There were brilliant students and laggards who showed little interest in academic subjects. More than two hundred students were in my graduating class. The two teachers whose seriousness and concern for conveying information were important influences on me were Madison Tignor, an English teacher, and Clyde McDuffie, a Latin teacher.

Tignor was a member of Shiloh Baptist Church to which my family belonged. My father was the chairman of the Deacon Board that included my uncle. My uncle's role after the conclusion of the sermon in the Sunday morning service was to stand in the aisle near the pulpit in his checkered sport coat and summery necktie to welcome the penitents who wished to join our church and to greet those persons who were transferring their church affiliation. My mother could never convince her brother to buy a respectable suit, like my father and I wore, from Lansburgh or Hecht, reputable department stores. My uncle, who had a deep affection for both my mother and his brother-in-law, remained unmoved by her appeals and our embarrassment.

Tignor was appointed director of the Sunday school that offered Bible study classes for youngsters an hour before the regular church service began at 11:00 a.m. I was chosen to be the pianist for the singing of hymns by the assembled students. Tignor (Tiggy, as my friend Clifford called him) was a stickler for correct grammatical usage and spelling in his high school classes. A misspelled word on an exam paper or book report would result in having five points deducted from the student's score. His obsession with correctness led, after several years in his position in the Sunday school, to his resignation. He refused to use the biblical material provided by a black publisher because there were too many excursions into ungrammatical English for his taste.

My mother had an anthology containing songs and folk songs from different countries. *The Laurel Song Book*, a gray, oversized volume with a rather thick cover that we kept in the piano bench, was probably purchased by her when she was in high school. I knew that she enjoyed hearing the songs that she was familiar with. When there was nothing to do before going to bed on Sunday evenings, I would begin to play my favorite songs from the book first. One by one, my mother, father, and grandmother would file into the parlor, leaving whatever they had been doing, to hum or sing along, standing behind me as I repeated the music several times. Then I would play dozens of hymns for them from a hymnal that I still have.

Both semesters of my fourth-year Latin class focused primarily on Virgil's *Aeneid*. The fascinating aspects and the tangential issues in this formidable work were explored by McDuffie. He discussed the derivation and origins of English words as well. In a classroom that had about thirty seats, only a couple were unoccupied. The theme of duty versus personal desire made a strong impression on me. In my small room at home was a beautiful, shiny, black rocking chair, one of three pieces of furniture. It was my favorite seat for considering matters of extreme gravity.

There are numerous high schools named after Paul Laurence Dunbar in the South and Midwest. Dunbar became known as the first black poet to achieve national recognition. Praised by a white literary critic, William Dean Howells, for his dialect poems, Dunbar was unsuccessful in achieving an equal renown for his serious works—short stories, novels, and a play. The recitation of his poetry in English classes and assemblies in the schools that I attended in Washington, DC, was limited to one or two poems in dialect. Today, these poems appear to be frivolous period works. Dunbar's relationship with his wife has been scrutinized and deplored by feminists in recent years.

Cadet Corps

Each of the three black high schools in Washington, DC, had a cadet corps. A retired U.S. Army colonel was in charge of the cadet corps at Dunbar High School. Regular army rifles were used in drills held in the armory, the basement area of the school. Every boy in the school was required to be a member of a company designated by the letters *A*, *B*, *C*, and *F*. The companies assembled twice a week at 3:00 p.m. after the end of the school day. Dark blue uniforms were worn on these days. Company commanders and staff officers wore a leather harness across their chest to which a blunt sword could be attached at the belt level.

On national holidays the companies would participate in a parade down the entire length of Pennsylvania Avenue, saluting the politicians in the grandstand along the route at the command "Eyes right." Promotions from the rank of private to that of corporal or sergeant were made at the beginning of the eleventh grade. Company officers and staff officers were announced in the fall of one's senior year. Promotions were presumed to be based on an exam and on the academic standing of the cadet.

A drill competition for all of the black high schools was held annually in the late spring at Griffith Stadium. The owner of the Washington Senators, Clark Griffith, had vowed to keep black players out of the major leagues. But he did not hesitate to rent his stadium on Sundays to the teams of the Negro Baseball League when no American League games were scheduled on those days.

Classes were suspended in the high schools on the day of the competition. It was a carnival-like event. Just inside the entrance of the stadium in the passageway leading to the box seats behind home plate and the right field foul line, cadets and their friends filled the area. Balloons floated and hawkers selling hot dogs and Cracker Jacks peddled their wares to the few with small change to spare.

After each company from all of the high schools had demonstrated its finesse in proscribed drill routines, a mock assault on the grass of the stadium followed. Instructors at the far end of the enclosure in front of the right field wall fired blanks at the approaching attackers who relied on flanking maneuvers to surround the defenders. The winning company achieved bragging rights for their high school.

For some undisclosed reason I was not promoted from a sergeant in Company B to the staff position that I felt was assured. Academically, I was in the upper 1 percent of my class. I had been prepared for the written exam based on army manuals by a retired army soldier, Sergeant Robinson, who lived in a small house around the corner of our block. I was convinced that there had been a gross mistake in marking the exam or of mixing my grade with that of another person. I have always known when I have done well on an exam.

Becoming a captain in the cadet corps was a dream that I had envisioned for two years. After I learned that I had not received this promotion, my father met with Colonel Atwood and informed him in no uncertain terms that his decision vis-à-vis my promotion was unacceptable. I refused to continue in the cadet program that had positioned friends in enviable ranks. This disappointment combined with other incidents in the high school effectively shored up my eagerness to attend a college outside of Washington, DC. The cadet corps debacle became one of the strongest motivating factors in my entire life. It colored gray the affection that I had for my alma mater.

Assemblies

At Dunbar High School there were assemblies in the auditorium about once a month for all students. During one assembly, Cortez Peters Sr., the black world speed-typing champion, demonstrated his phenomenal facility and accuracy. He and his son are considered to be the greatest typists of all time. Their technique is still the basis for teaching this skill. Another cousin of ours, Laura Robinson, taught in the Cortez Peters Business College in Washington, DC. That school has produced forty-five thousand graduates.

When I was in the tenth grade, someone informed Miss Mary Europe, the music teacher in Dunbar High School, that I played the piano. (I had played a solo work on my graduation program at Garnet-Patterson Junior High School.) Miss Europe was the sister of Lt. James Reese Europe, the celebrated bandleader whose ensemble was first embraced in Europe by the French at the end of World War I. When they returned to the United States, they were accorded a triumphant reception.

Miss Europe asked me to play something for an assembly on a half hour's notice. After some deliberation about what I could remember and what would be appropriate, I played George Hamer's "Majesty of the Deep." The response from my fellow students was enthusiastic. This piano work remains one of the most popular teaching pieces in the catalog of Theodore Presser.

A year later, prior to the arrival of an Indian dignitary who had been invited to address an assembly, Miss Europe again asked me to play something with no prior notice. After my performance of the "Juba Dance" by Nathaniel Dett, the entire school body erupted vociferously with foot stomping and whistles—a reception more like one accorded a rock star than a classical performer. I became an instant celebrity in the school. The rhythmic element, not the melodic tunefulness, in the Dett dance sparked the effusive response from my classmates.

· 2 ·

College and Career

CAREER CONSIDERATION

$\mathcal{I}$ did not decide to pursue a career in music until I had begun to think about where I wanted to go for my college degree. My father never suggested that I consider becoming a physician, although one of my favorite retreats (to escape the recurrent calls for help from my mother who would be working in the kitchen) was my father's office. I enjoyed twirling myself in his swivel chair.

Nearly all of his professional colleagues were doctors and dentists from Jamaica, Trinidad, and Barbados. All of them treated me with a little deference. A few adults in our neighborhood had been calling me "Doc" for a long time.

I wrote to Harvard University to obtain a catalog of their curriculum. When the slim red book arrived, I discovered that instrumental music was not offered in its music department. My piano teacher, Mrs. Mitchell, suggested to my mother that I apply for admission to Oberlin College. After reading about Oberlin, I discovered that it had all of the advantages of an excellent college and the facilities of a first-rate music school. It was rated by the *Chicago Tribune* as the best coed college in the country.

In the winter of 1937 the director of admissions from Oberlin College came to our home to interview me. When he appeared skeptical about the prospect of a fourteen year old entering the college as a freshman, my mother thoughtfully assured him that I had a strong interest in sports. Her statements were intended to convince him that I was a normal boy, not a prodigy.

During my final semester at Dunbar High School, my piano teacher, Mrs. Lillian Mitchell, decided that I should give a solo piano recital. (Each spring the advanced piano students in the Junior Department of Music played in a public concert held in Andrew Rankin Memorial Chapel of Howard University. It was attended mostly by relatives of the students.) This was an unprecedented decision by Miss Nickerson and Mrs. Mitchell. My solo piano recital in June consisted of works by Bach, Beethoven (Pathetique Sonata), Chopin, Ibert, and Debussy played on a Steinway D Concert Grand. For this event I wore my Sunday best—a dark blue jacket, white flannel trousers, and white shoes. My treasured Panama hat was left at home.

Yearbook photo from Dunbar High School in Washington, DC, 1937

GEORGE THEOPHILUS WALKER, JR.

*When he is at the piano, Walker
Makes every key become a talker.*
Tennis, Rex, Basketball, Handball,
Ping-pong
To be a concert pianist

Classmate quote from Dunbar yearbook, 1937

HOWARD UNIVERSITY FACULTY

The faculty of the Department of Music at Howard University was the best of any black university. It included the pianist Hazel Harrison, a pupil of Egon Petri; Todd Duncan of *Porgy and Bess* fame; Roy Tibbs, a pianist, organist, and husband of Lillian Evanti, a soprano who had sung operatic roles in Europe; and Cecil Cohen, a piano teacher who had composed a few songs. Lulu Vere Childers, a graduate of the Oberlin Conservatory of Music in voice, founded the music department and was its chairperson.

Andrew Rankin Memorial Chapel was the site for the annual artist series. I had the opportunity of hearing two Juilliard instructors, Alton Jones and James Friskin, in piano recitals as well as Hazel Harrison, Egon Petri, and the cellist Raya Garbousova. Roy Tibbs appeared with the National Symphony Orchestra under Hans Kindler in a solid, but rhythmically squarish performance of the Liszt Piano Concerto no. 1.

Occasionally my parents would forsake Sunday worship in our church to attend the chapel service at Howard University. The student choir, supplementing the nondenominational devotionals, produced rich, sonorous harmonies in the reverberant acoustic. Dr. Howard Thurman, dean of the chapel, was the primary speaker in these services.

He spoke with a quiet eloquence. My mother recalled a mesmerizing moment in the beginning of the exegesis of a sermon when he described the falling of a leaf.

Thurman had met Gandhi in India. When he left Howard University to become dean of the chapel at Boston University, his conviction about nonviolence as a desirable approach to resolve conflict influenced a young graduate student in the university, Dr. Martin Luther King. *Life* magazine called Dr. Thurman one of the twelve most influential religious leaders in America.

When Warner Lawson was appointed dean of the School of Music at Howard University, as well as choir director (William Grant Still was one of the unsuccessful applicants), he was instructed by members of the music department to make the acquaintance of the Walker family immediately. My father's ties to the Department of Music at Howard and to the president of the university, Mordecai Johnson, were significant. Lawson dutifully paid us a visit. I played the Valse Oubliée of Liszt and the Poulenc Toccata for him on our Chickering grand piano. Under Lawson's leadership the Howard University Choir achieved national prominence. Jessye Norman became the most conspicuous graduate of the music department.

My piano teacher, Mrs. Mitchell, persuaded my parents to allow me to go with her to a recital by Roland Hayes in the chapel of Howard University. Roland Hayes was the first black classical singer to achieve an international reputation. Ordinarily, I would have been shuttled off to bed at 8:00 p.m. After the program, Mrs. Mitchell led me behind the stage where an emotionally drained tenor was waiting to greet his admirers. Although we were among the first of those who wanted to shake his hand, my teacher diffidently allowed others to forge ahead of us. We were the last persons to be introduced to him. By that time he seemed reluctant to talk to us.

Mrs. Mitchell was less successful in convincing my mother to let me hear a recital by Ignace Paderewski in Constitution Hall in downtown Washington, DC. Segregated seating was offered to black patrons. The Daughters of the American Revolution and the manager of Constitution Hall had established this reprehensible policy for all concerts in this hall. My mother refused to consider the idea of my attending a concert there under those conditions. She was adamantly opposed to discrimination. When Todd Duncan was chosen to sing

Porgy in Gershwin's opera *Porgy and Bess*, she strongly voiced her objection to his role as a crap-shooting cripple crawling on his knees. The music was less significant to her than the scurrilous ghetto setting of this American work.

SUMMER CAMP

In the summer of 1934 when I was twelve years old, I attended a camp in North Brookfield, Massachusetts. The head administrator of Camp Atwater, Mr. John Burr, was the director of athletics at Howard University. Camp Atwater was the first and most prestigious camp for black youths. Boys from several states came for two weeks or a month to live in wooden cabins, to swim and paddle in canoes and rowboats, to play baseball on a field encrusted with patches of prickly weeds, and to play tennis on beige-colored clay courts. I was in a contingent of four or five boys who boarded a train from Washington, DC, to go to Springfield, Massachusetts. From Springfield we went to Brookfield.

The experiences that I had at this camp contributed to the development of my self-confidence and poise. I became fascinated with tennis. It remains my primary hobby. When my parents drove up to Massachusetts to bring me home after a month in Camp Atwater, they met with the director before we left. Mr. Burr told them that I was the runner-up for the best-all-around camper award. I was also the mumbly-peg champion after beating my friend, Raymond, who had taught me the game and its sequence of knife throwing.

OBERLIN COLLEGE

When I received the letter of admission to Oberlin College, I had already decided to turn down an offer from Howard University for a four-year scholarship. I applied to Oberlin for a scholarship. An audition was arranged with the director of the conservatory, Dr. Frank Shaw.

My father, who disliked driving, persuaded his friend, Huver Brown, a lawyer with a wonderfully droll sense of humor, to accompany him and myself for the trip to Oberlin, Ohio. Mr. Brown would often regale us at home with episodes of hilarious malfeasance by some of his clients.

There were a few scary moments when my father's Buick balked at the task of climbing the hilly streets in Pittsburgh. This city was our only stop. We entered a drugstore for a drink. Sitting on the tall stools at the soda fountain, Mr. Brown and I asked for sodas. I was amazed to hear my father order a "phosphate." I had never heard of one before. But the soda jerker understood the request.

I played Bach and Brahms for Shaw. Then he asked me to sight-read a hymn. Since I was accustomed to doing this in Sunday school, it posed no problem for me. (I had to remember not to double the bass of the hymn, which I did to increase the sonority of the upright piano in our Sunday school room.) Finally, he asked me to turn my back while he played random notes from different registers of the piano for me to identify. No one had ever tested my ear before. I found pitch recognition easy.

A few weeks later I received a letter from Oberlin College stating that I would receive a scholarship that would cover my tuition, room, and board. I became the only black student in my conservatory class, one of five black students in my entire college class, and, at fifteen years old, the youngest student in the whole school.

The trip by train to Oberlin, Ohio, in the fall of 1937 was a tedious seven-hour coach journey. The bench-styled seats were fairly straight and stiff. It was impossible to curl up in a comfortable sleeping position. When the train reached Akron, Ohio, prior to its final destination in Cleveland, it kept backing in and out of the yard for an hour while changing tracks and engines. Taking a bus from Cleveland to Oberlin was the final leg of this miserably slow trip. If my parents experienced any anxiety about my departure to college without any friends, they never showed it.

I had requested a single room in the Men's Building, an old wooden structure that could have been condemned then, despite having a rusty fire escape outside of my window. The closet-sized room on the second floor contained a bed and an old, well-scarred desk. In the large first-floor lobby of the building there was a dilapidated grand piano, a couple of well-worn armchairs, and a warped table tennis table. In the basement of the building was a room used for an hour of dancing during the week after dinner was finished in the dormitories that served meals.

Music was provided for this "rec" (short for recreation) period by a student combo. Listening occasionally from the steps above the entrance of the room to the sounds emanating from the basement was my first exposure to live jazz.

I was eager to demonstrate my ability as a tennis player by entering a tournament in the freshman orientation period prior to the beginning of the fall semester. A loss to another freshman who said that he was the New Jersey state junior champion was hardly consoling. However, in the spring I occupied the number two spot behind him on the freshman tennis team. The following spring, on a cold, wintry March day, I witnessed Don McNeill of Kenyon College defeat our number one player. A few years later McNeill became the United States tennis champion by beating Bobby Riggs in the National Clay Championship and the United States Open in Forest Hills, New York.

Conservatory Curriculum

Incoming freshmen were allowed to choose a teacher for their major subject in the Conservatory of Music. I was intrigued to read in the conservatory catalog that Professor David Moyer had studied in Germany. Although I didn't know anything at that time about Busoni, his teacher, I requested Mr. Moyer. His background seemed to have been more cosmopolitan than that of the other piano faculty.

Students majoring in instrumental music received two half-hour lessons a week. Piano majors were assigned rooms in Rice Memorial Hall (Warner Hall Annex) for four hours of daily practice. These rooms, equipped with small grand pianos, had porous walls. Walking down the corridor on the second or third floor was to venture in a cacophony of sound that made individual works virtually indecipherable.

There were challenges for me to overcome. In high school I was only able to practice for a half hour a day before breakfast and the ensuing walk to school. It was daunting to realize that I was expected to spend four hours each day in these rooms. Sitting on unbearably hard chairs to practice for my piano lessons was physically painful. The height of most of the chairs was another issue. Every day I tried to find the lowest chair from the rooms that were not in use. I had found that by sitting lower I did not experience pain in my neck from bending over the piano.

In the catalog of the Oberlin Conservatory of Music was a required list of works to be studied by instrumental majors. For each of the four years in the bachelor of music program the graded list increased in difficulty from the first year to the fourth year. Piano majors progressed from Bach's Two and Three Part Inventions (Sinfonias) to the *Well-Tempered Clavier* and the Suites, in that order. Since I had never played the Two Part Inventions, my progress up the ladder seemed unbearably slow, especially when I could discern fragments of the Chopin Scherzo in C-sharp Minor filtered from a practice room in the annex. I could hardly wait to learn that wonderful piece.

Three years of music theory were mandated for all conservatory students. Dr. Frank Shaw apparently decided to trim his budget by having a senior piano major teach the seven or eight students in my first-year theory class. The result of this decision was a casual dispersion by the senior of the rules of common practice harmony that were unsupported by the use of a textbook. The student-teacher was an affable chap with no affectation. But we didn't learn anything thoroughly to prepare us for the final exam at the end of the year. It was customary to have the theory students from all of the instructors seated in the recital space of Warner Concert Hall for these tests.

In my second year of theory, an inadequate Juilliard textbook by Wedge was used. George Lillich, an organ teacher, was a full-time faculty member with whom I had theory for three years. (I elected to take Fugue and Canon in my fourth year.) He tried to instill effort and enthusiasm into a phlegmatic group of instrumental and voice majors by rallying them to their assignments as a coach would attempt to pump up his athletes. Grading on a curve, he made sure each year that I would not have the highest grade in the final exams even though I was the best student in the class. The final exam determined the grade for the course.

I had chosen organ as my minor concentration. Arthur Croley, an instructor from Fisk University in Nashville, Tennessee, had been hired to teach at Oberlin for one year. He became my first organ teacher. I had never touched an organ before coming to the conservatory. The excellent progress that I made was due in part to my facility as a pianist. Even so, it came as a surprise to me when Croley proposed that I play a joint recital in the spring of my freshman year with an organ major, Robert Owen.

Years later, Owen became the director of music at Christ Church in Bronxville, New York. He was the consultant for the enormous Flentrop Organ that was designed to be installed in Carnegie Hall. When Isaac Stern mounted a protest against having an organ in this venerable institution (he was afraid that the acoustics of Carnegie would be adversely affected), the organ was given to the State University of New York in Purchase. I saw Bob for the first time since we were students at Oberlin when he attended the premiere of my Violin Concerto in the highly regarded acoustic in Purchase.

David Moyer, my piano teacher, assigned two Mendelssohn études in F major and a minor from op. 104b for me to learn. He told me that Rachmaninoff played them. As my playing of the études improved, he considered having me play them on a student recital in my freshman year. This would have been unusual. Then, he decided that I would make a stronger impression if I waited until the beginning of the fall semester of my sophomore year to play them. My performance did indeed create a mild sensation. With each succeeding appearance on these student programs, I concluded the recitals.

Housing Problem

A housing shortage at Oberlin presented a dilemma for male students returning for their sophomore year. A new upper class dorm, Noah Hall, could not accommodate all of the students who wanted to live there. At a meeting in the spring of my freshman year, straws were drawn out of a hat in the dean's office in Bosworth Hall to determine who would live in Noah Hall. I was one of three black students in my college class who failed to qualify for the available rooms. We were forced to consider the option of living separately in private homes in the town.

Fortunately, two single middle-aged black women, Ms. Woods and Ms. Duncan, decided to convert their home on Elm Street into a dorm. It was called "the Arches." The structure housed five men on the second floor. I had the only single room. The women lived on the first floor. Ms. Woods and Ms. Duncan provided a warm, parental atmosphere. Nevertheless, I felt isolated from the rest of my class. I was the only conservatory student in this group.

Since there were five men living in the Arches, it seemed perfectly natural to form a basketball team to play in the intramural league. With the exception of Jimmy Malone, who was the star quarter miler on the Oberlin College track team, none of the other three fellows had any athletic ability. The team played haphazardly, losing the first two of five games in the tournament.

Exasperated by the failure of my teammates to pass the ball to me, I resolved to shoot whenever I was able to handle the ball. A hook shot after a pivot that I tried one time resulted in ten consecutive points in each of the remaining games. Our house won the league championship. At the end of the academic year, three of the five students in the Arches decided to move to Noah Hall for the following fall term.

Toward the end of the second semester, one of the fellows in the Arches broached the idea of having a party before final exams began. We obtained the approval of Ms. Woods and Ms. Duncan. Several girls in the college and a few of the friendly divinity students were invited. Before the party ended, one of my classmates persuaded Avery Parrish, a jazz pianist whom he had met, to play something on the ugly, snaggled-tooth, yellow-keyed upright piano in the living room. (I could never bring myself to touch it.) How Parrish managed to produce recognizable pitches on this abandoned relic was incredulous. His playing of "After Hours," a famous blues song that he had composed (I had never heard it before) with flat, twisting untrained fingers punching out a stream of repeated notes was eye-opening.

When I moved to Noah Hall, I had two roommates. The first, Kenneth Clement, had been the president of his black high school class in Cleveland, Ohio. He was a tiresomely verbose sophomore who liked to speak about the faux pas (probably the only French that he knew, adding an "s" for the plural) of others in every conversation. Although he didn't distinguish himself academically at Oberlin, he became, after graduating from the Medical School at Howard University, a well-known surgeon and political activist in Cleveland. My second roommate, Bob Turpin, was his cousin—a much more pleasant, good-humored fellow who became a dentist.

Tennis Tournaments

During the summer, when I returned to Washington, DC, I played tennis every day on the red clay courts of Banneker Junior High School. It was about a twenty-five-minute walk from my home to the recreation area. The courts were rolled every morning. By late afternoon they were well-scuffed from continuous play on them.

After turning seventeen, I entered the citywide tennis tournament for black junior players for the second time. I won both the singles and doubles title. Eddie Davis, the director of the tennis program at Banneker, who was always friendly and accommodating, pocketed the trophy money given to him by the Department of Interior. After I made several inquiries about the trophy that I should have received, he offered me a blue tinted ashtray in its place. Fortunately for him, I didn't tell my father about his theft.

My father agreed to drive me to Hampton, Virgina, where the ATA (American Tennis Association) was hosting the National Tennis Championship tournament for black players. I expected to enter the junior tennis tournament as the champion from the District of Columbia. After we arrived in Hampton, it rained continuously for two days. The clay courts were soaked. With the prospect of more rain on a third day, we threw in the towel and returned home. I was very disappointed.

But I did see Dr. Reginald Weir play part of his first match. A former captain of the City College of New York tennis team, he became the first black tennis player to compete in the National Indoor Championship of the USTA (United States Tennis Association), the white-only organization. He was featured on the front page of the *New York Times* after defeating the reigning world champion, Jaroslav Drobny, a Czech, in a match at Forest Hills, New York. Weir's father, who taught violin, lived in Washington, DC.

Piano Recitals

Instrumental piano majors in the Oberlin Conservatory of Music were required to play before the entire piano faculty in the spring of their sophomore year. The exam was adjudicated in Warner Concert Hall. After playing the Waldstein Sonata of Beethoven and receiving high grades from all of the teachers, I felt dissatisfied with my performance. Sitting on the steps of the annex on a bright, sunny afternoon, I decided to alter my approach to practicing the piano by concentrating on having complete control of every work that I performed in public.

When I expressed a desire to play another recital in Washington, DC, the following winter, my father made all of the arrangements for a program in our church. A Steinway D concert grand was rented from Kitts, the local music store. The program included works that I had played on Oberlin student recitals (Bach-Busoni Toccata in D Minor, Beethoven's Waldstein Sonata) and concluded with the Polonaise in A-flat by Chopin. The day after the concert my father gave me $250 in cash, the entire proceeds from the recital. He had personally sold most of the tickets and had solicited everyone he knew to publicize this concert. I was happy to see some of my high school friends afterward.

In the audience was a piano student who was studying music at West Virginia Institute, a black college. He was so impressed by my concert that he begged the chairman of the music department in West Virginia to have me appear on their lyceum series. This was arranged.

The recital that I played at West Virginia Institute was my first professional concert and the first one played outside of Washington, DC. The reviewer for a newspaper in Charleston, West Virginia, wrote that the concert was more than worth the distance that he had travelled to hear it. The chairman of the music department attempted to short-change my fee. But a letter from my father that threatened to expose him brought the balance to me quickly.

Oberlin Theological Seminary

In a brief, casual conversation with Henry Booker, a black organ major from Washington, DC, who was graduating from Oberlin College at the end of my second year, I learned that his position as the organist of the Oberlin Theological Seminary would be available in my junior year. I applied for the position with his recommendation and was accepted. It was my very first job—one that paid me a small sum each month.

The Oberlin Theological Seminary was regarded at that time as one of the top five divinity schools in the country. A two-manual organ was the centerpiece of a small, intimate chapel. Every weekday at 8:00 a.m. there was a service lasting a half hour in Fairchild Chapel. My responsibility was to play two hymns and to conclude the service with a brief organ response, which I improvised. It was a cherished pleasure to use the key to the chapel at night to practice improvising in the solitary space on the organ as J. S. Bach might have done.

After my freshman year, I ate all of my meals in the dining room of the seminary with the prospective degree candidates and undergraduate students from the college. I could observe their personalities. A few of these "theologs," as the seminary graduate students were called, earned their keep by waiting tables. Hoisting large platters above their head, they pushed precariously through the swinging door that led to the kitchen. The most adroit of these waiters was Cash.

One of the theologs was Gardner C. Taylor. Taylor was a large man who appeared to be comfortably introspective. I was somewhat surprised to learn from comments made by other graduate students in the seminary that he was already an impressive preacher. Although I had made friends with several of these students, I never had a conversation with him.

After obtaining his divinity degree from Oberlin, Taylor eventually became the pastor of the Concord Baptist Church in Brooklyn, New York, which had a congregation of fourteen thousand. His reputation skyrocketed. Taylor became known as the greatest black preacher in the country and has received over one hundred honorary degrees. He is also considered to have been a mentor of Dr. Martin Luther King. The Medal of Freedom was bestowed upon him by President Clinton in 2000.

There was no interest in the musical part of the morning service by anyone. The presiding minister for that particular week simply gave me the hymns that would be sung. The divinity school dean was cold, uncommunicative, and bureaucratic. None of the fledgling pastors ever commented on my organ playing, although some of the responses at the end of the morning services must have seemed strange to them. (I experimented with contemporary harmonies that extended common practice tonality.) However, one of the graduate students, Albert Faurot, was a pianist who had become a missionary. We often talked about music. He attended my senior recital. He would listen to me when I would practice portions of the Tschaikowsky Piano Concerto on the upright piano in the dining hall where we ate.

Faurot had gone to China, moving inland when the Japanese occupied the area in which he resided, before he came to Oberlin. He taught piano to a Chinese student, Frederic Ming Chang, who came to the United States and enrolled in the music department of Indiana University. After receiving a master's degree, Ming obtained a position in Seton Hall University in South Orange, New Jersey. We became acquainted when he attended one of my piano recitals in the public library in Newark, New Jersey.

Faurot went to Japan after World War II and then to the Philippines, where he taught at Silliman University in Dumaguete City. He published a thoroughly researched book, *Concert Piano Repertoire*, that reflects a firsthand knowledge of piano literature. This compendium differs from the vague and sycophantic commentaries of David Dubal, a Juilliard instructor. A second book, *Team Piano Repertoire*, was published with the collaboration of his student, Ming Chang. About two years before Faurot's death, I saw Albert again. He played my Piano Sonata no. 2 at the Riverside Church in New York and on several programs in this country.

Near the end of the academic year (1940), I was asked by the dean of the seminary to provide a program of choral music for the seminary students. At the beginning of that year I had joined the Oberlin Acapella Choir—to my parents' amusement. They were convinced that I didn't have a voice worthy of any vocal ensemble.

I was able to corral a few friends from the choir to sing on the program that I conducted. Included in the program was a short choral work that I had composed. This was my second attempt at composing. In the fall of my freshman year, when I was fifteen, I surprised one of my classmates who liked jazz by writing a song that he admitted was about as good as one of his Ellington favorites.

Organ Decision

Arthur Poister, the organ teacher with whom I studied for two years, had played all of the organ works of J. S. Bach from memory on a series of concerts before coming to Oberlin. He gave me programs from those recitals. During my junior year he assigned to me the Passacaglia from Leo Sowerby's Organ Symphony. It has a long theme with over thirty variations. I learned the work quickly and performed it from memory as the final work on a student recital a few weeks later. Dr. Frank Shaw, the director of the conservatory, was so impressed with my performance of a contemporary work that he came backstage before I left to congratulate me. It was highly unusual to have a twentieth-century work by a living American composer performed at these recitals. Invariably, organ majors played standard works with the music on the rack.

I could not visualize myself as a church organist who would be responsible for conducting a choir every week. Yet it was difficult for me to tell my teacher, Arthur Poister, that I would not be taking organ in my senior year. My reason for discontinuing organ lessons was that I wanted to concentrate on becoming a better pianist. I was also curious about how composition was taught.

At the beginning of my first semester in the conservatory, I had a brief conversation with a classmate who told me that composition was his major. It had not occurred to me that someone would choose a major that was neither instrumental or vocal. When I asked Bob Crane what he was composing, he said, "A fandango." Never having heard of a "fandango," I was puzzled, but also intrigued.

I officially severed my connection to organ playing in the summer of 1940. I had played the organ for the junior choir of my church and had access to the organ on weekdays. My farewell gesture was to play the great D Major Prelude and Fugue of Bach from memory in the sanctuary, which was devoid of any presence other than myself. Although I had not played it for a several weeks, it went perfectly.

Beginning Composition

I decided to take composition for the first semester of my senior year. Normand Lockwood, the composition teacher, was a rather large, heavy-set man with a massive black mustache. He had studied in Europe and had been a recipient of a Prix de Rome Fellowship. He was appointed on his return to the United States to an assistant professorship at Oberlin.

In my first lessons with him he asked me to write several unharmonized melodies, then harmonized melodies, and eventually songs using texts of my choice. Relying on my knowledge from high school of English literature, I selected poems by Shelley and Byron. I also chose to set to music a rather sentimental poem by Paul Laurence Dunbar. This setting with the title "Response" was tinkered with for a long time before it was published and eventually recorded.

Lockwood introduced me to a few songs of Charles Ives and to the Symphony of Psalms by Stravinsky. Seated at the piano, he would intone the melody softly as he searched for the approximate harmonies from the piano score. The grade that I received at the end of the semester indicated that he was not overly impressed by my ability.

Toward the end of the second semester, after having discontinued my composition lessons, I composed my first solo piano work.

The original title, "Danse Exotique," was changed to "Caprice" before it was published. It is a short virtuoso composition with a strong rhythmic character. After hearing a work of Horowitz called "Danse Excentrique," I decided to compose a more demanding technical work. The octaves at the end are difficult. The inclusion of imitation and the harmonic content make the "Caprice" much more intricate than the "Danse" of Horowitz.

Lockwood was a prolific composer. The music of his that I have heard lacks individuality and is rather amorphous. He was forced to resign his position as an assistant professor at Oberlin after an alleged affair with a student. A rumor circulated after his dismissal that he was going to study with Stravinsky. But Stravinsky never taught anybody. It was quite a coincidence to be paired with Lockwood on an LP that was recorded by C.R.I. (Composers Recordings Inc.) in 1983.

Concert Artists

The Artist Recital Series of Oberlin College presented the most distinguished performers in the world of music. In Finney Chapel, I was privileged to hear Kreisler, Rachmaninoff, Feuermann, Kipnis, John Charles Thomas, Marian Anderson, Tibbett, Horowitz, Serkin, Gieseking, Francescatti, and other lesser luminaries. Poister introduced me to his teacher, Marcel Dupre, after his recital in Finney Chapel. He told Dupre that he hoped that I would at some future date become his pupil. That was before I had decided to discontinue my organ studies.

Rachmaninoff came to Oberlin to play a recital in Finney Chapel in my sophomore year. He began by playing the Bach French Suite in E. I decided to stand up for the second half of the program in the balcony overlooking the stage. The acoustics in the chapel were muddy even with a full house.

His position at the piano for this concert was unusual. He bent forward from the waist with elbows slightly splayed out at an angle from his torso. A wedding ring was on the fourth finger of his left hand. There were quite a few clinkers, notes that were not cleanly struck that produced an indeterminate pitch. His playing was unlike that of Horowitz, who allowed the music to unfold in the moment. Rachmaninoff's playing was characterized by a calculated determination of the shape of each work. There was no stylistic connection to the music of any period. Exaggerated ritards, willful dynamics, and tempi were intentional. This playing was clearly idiosyncratic.

In the winter of 1939 Mr. Moyer, my piano teacher, invited me to attend a Cleveland Orchestra concert with him and his wife on which Rachmaninoff would be playing the Beethoven Piano Concerto no. 1 and his own Variations on a Theme of Paganini. Mr. Moyer drove us from Oberlin to Severance Hall for the evening performance. We had seats in the balcony.

With the orchestra seated for the piano concerto, Rachmaninoff emerged from backstage. Walking so slowly, he appeared to take forever to reach the piano bench. His feet seemed encased in size thirteen shoes. But from the first entrance of the piano in the Beethoven concerto, a striking authority exuded from his playing. The slow movement of the Beethoven projected the arch of the melodic line boldly. His own Variations on a Theme of Paganini crackled with incisiveness and rhythmic energy. This was a memorable concert.

As we drove out of the parking garage, Rachmaninoff's chauffeured limousine pulled up beside us at a stoplight. Rachmaninoff was in the backseat directly across from where I was sitting. I tried to convey my admiration for his performance by gesturing to him with hands clenched together as he looked out of the window. When his limousine moved ahead of us, I could not be sure that he smiled in return. This concert was a wonderful gift from my piano teacher, David Moyer.

I had developed a considerable curiosity about piano playing methods and piano pedagogy. Reading reviews of New York recitals found in publications like *Musical America* and listening to 78 rpm records also became quite fascinating to me. I discovered the first recording by Vladimir Horowitz of the Liszt Sonata in B Minor in the conservatory record library. Both the music and the performance of it were captivating. After informing Mr. Moyer about the 78 rpm disc, I began to learn the sonata. (I became aware of the rhythmical distortions and wrong notes that marred the accuracy of his recording.)

Fortuitously, I read in the *Cleveland Plain Dealer* in 1939 that Horowitz, who had taken a sabbatical from his concertizing, was returning to the concert stage. He had been engaged to play a recital in Cleveland. I was determined to hear this concert. Taking the bus from Oberlin to Cleveland by myself, I arrived in time to buy a seat in the balcony of the Cleveland venue. The number of persons in this section could be counted on two hands. The parquet was not completely filled. But the performances of a Mendelssohn Prelude and Fugue in F minor, Schumann Phantasie and Toccata, four Chopin études, four Debussy études, and Horowitz's Carmen Fantasy remain indelible.

The following year Horowitz was engaged to play on the Artist Recital series at Oberlin. I made an appointment to see Dr. Shaw to obtain permission to interview Horowitz for the student newspaper. In denying my request it was clear that Shaw, who called Horowitz a "genius," was not comfortable with having a black student making contact with Toscanini's son-in-law. For Horowitz's concert in Finney Chapel, I managed to switch my assigned seat in Finney Chapel with another student. I had a full frontal view of the keyboard from the second row left center.

It was a little unnerving to see the right hand of Horowitz trembling as he began the first movement of the Piano Sonata, op. 31, no. 3, of Beethoven, and the slender fourth finger flattened at the first joint on the black keys. He inhaled audibly before beginning phrases and his head wagged back and forth as he negotiated passages at the extremes of the keyboard. After the concert I went backstage to obtain an autograph. His wife, Wanda, dressed in black, was standing protectively by the side of the table where he was seated. He turned a few pages of the Schirmer edition of the Chopin sonatas that I gave him and remarked, as he looked at one page, that he was unaware of a particular marking in my score.

Following the Beethoven sonata on the program that Horowitz gave was the Schumann Arabesque, the Chopin Piano Sonata no. 2, the Sonetto 104 del Petrarch, *Au Bord d'une Source*, *Feux Follets* of Liszt, and six études by Jebolinsky. Years later Horowitz was highly complimentary of the audiences for his Oberlin concerts. Some of his New York recitals in Carnegie Hall attracted less attentive listeners who could be extremely annoying as they rattled programs or whispered during the quiet sections of a work.

Senior Recital

Toward the end of my junior year, the conservatory faculty voted to have me play a concerto with the Conservatory Orchestra as a part of my senior recital. My choice of the Tschaikowsky Piano Concerto no. 1 coincided with the exposure given the work by a recording made by Artur Rubinstein. Subsequently, an LP by Horowitz and Toscanini became a best-seller.

George T. Walker Scores In Senior Performance

CLEVELAND, O., Mar. 13—Friday evening, in the Warner Concert Hall of the Oberlin Conservatory of Music, a capacity audience sat enthralled while the magic fingers of an 16-year-old boy wove a spell on the keys of a huge grand piano. The boy was George T. Walker, the occasion, his senior recital, and the consensus of opinion, that it was a splendid and artistic performance given by a Conservatory student in several years. His extremely difficult program consisted of the Bach-Busoni "Toccata in C Major," prelude, adagio, and fuge; the "Fantasy in C Major," by Schumann, allegro molto appassionata, majestico con energia, and lento moderato; dignified by the stirring Tchaikowsky "Concerto in E-Flat Minor," andante non troppo e molto maestoso, andante, semplice and allegro con fuoco, assisted by the Conservatory Orchestra. Incidentally, George played the entire program from memory.

After the recital, his piano teacher, Dr. Moyer, held a reception at his home for the Walker family and a few friends, and Saturday night, George did a bit of celebrating on his own with a party at the "Arches," the boys' dorm.

George's home is in Washington, D.C., and he has been studying the piano for thirteen years. He entered Oberlin when he was 14, and now, at the age when most of us are preparing to graduate from high school, he is preparing for graduation with honors from one of the best conservatories in the country.

S & S MUSIC CO.

Sales   RADIO   SERVICE

RECORDS FOR SALE

MIchigan 8018   415 Florida Avenue, N. W.

Program

George T. Walker, Jr.

Fantasie in C mi .... Mozart

Organ Toccata and Fugue in D mi Bach Tausig

Steinway Grand Piano

Courtesy of

I began my recital with the Busoni transcription of the Bach Organ Toccata in C Major. The second work on the program was the great Phantasie of Schumann that I had heard David Moyer play in a faculty recital the previous year. (These two works initiated Horowitz's Carnegie Hall concert in 1965 after his second sabbatical.) Every seat was taken in Warner Concert Hall for my recital. There were even standees. The concert, according to one newspaper, drew the largest attendance for that hall "within recent memory."

Serkin Concert

In my senior year Rudolf Serkin came to Oberlin. After practicing scales, arpeggios, and octaves for forty-five minutes in the morning in Warner Concert Hall, he continued to practice for additional hours in the afternoon in Finney Chapel. It was my good fortune to have walked past the chapel en route to dinner at the theological seminary when I heard the sound of a piano. (A year earlier the same scenario had occurred before the concert by Horowitz. When I went inside of the chapel, I saw him seated at the piano on the stage. He was talking with a piano tuner about voicing a few notes around middle C. When he was satisfied that the adjustments had been made, he played the Black Key Étude of Chopin from its beginning to the end. There was no practicing of anything after that.)

I stealthily entered the chapel. Serkin was practicing the Butterfly Étude of Chopin, which he played as an encore. Another person also heard the sound of the piano outside of the building. After entering the chapel, he stood beside me as I peered around one of the pillars supporting the balcony. Suddenly, Serkin stopped playing. He looked toward the back of the chapel and spotted us. Then he called out to ask if we could play something. He wanted to judge the acoustics of Finney Chapel.

I had no idea who the person was who was standing next to me. But he gave me a nudge with his elbow. I went up to the stage and played two of the Brahms-Paganini variations that I had just learned. In the evening, when I received my program for the concert, I was surprised to see that Serkin was concluding his recital with the Liszt-Paganini variations in a minor. His program began with Bach's Capriccio on the Departure of a Beloved Brother. That was followed by the Beethoven Piano Sonata op. 78. The subsequent set of variations by Reger seemed interminable.

PROGRAM

Saturday, June 7, 1941
at 10:00 a. m.

Part One

Lamento et Tarentelle, for clarinet - - - - *Greeler*
  Mr. McGinnis

Ballade in F minor - - - - - *Chopin*
  Mr. Skyrm

Ein junger Dichter denkt an die Geliebte - *Marx*
Der Jüngling an der Quelle - - *Schubert*
Ihre Stimme - - - - *Schumann*
  Mr. Numbers

Four Etudes Op. 25 - - - - *Chopin*
  G-sharp minor
  B minor
  C minor
  G-flat major
  Mr. Kleiman

Suite Italienne, for violin - - - - *Stravinsky*
  Introduzione
  Serenata
  Gavotta con due variazioni
  Minuetto e Finale
  Mr. Huber

Sonata, Op. 34, for two pianos - - - - *Brahms*
  Allegro non troppo
  Miss Crowell Mrs. Josephine Lyttle

Voluntary, for trombone and two pianos - *Robert Crane*
  Mr. Thomas Cramer Mr. Arthur Dann Mr. Ludwig Lenel

Danses, for harp and string orchestra - - *Debussy*
  Miss Mayfield and String Orchestra

PROGRAM

Saturday, June 7, 1941
at 8:30 p. m.

Part Two

Symphony, No. 2, for organ - - - - *Vierne*
  Allegro
  Mr. Green

Sonata, Op. 58 - - - - - *Chopin*
  Largo
  Finale
  Miss Van Slyke

Variations Symphoniques, for cello and piano - *Boëllmann*
  Miss Mudge Miss Crowell

Tarantella (Venezia e Napoli) - - - - *Liszt*
  Miss Koski

Concerto, Op. 77, for violin and orchestra - - *Brahms*
  Allegro non troppo
  Mr. Keff and Conservatory Orchestra

Dichterliebe - - - - - *Schumann*
  Im wunderschönen Monat Mai
  Wenn ich in deine Augen seh'
  Die Rose, die Lilie, die Taube, die Sonne
  Ich grolle nicht

Music, When Soft Voices Die - - - *Roger Quilter*
The Pretty Creature - - arr. by *H. Lane Wilson*
  Mr. McKelvy

Concerto in B-flat minor, for piano and orchestra - *Tchaikovsky*
  Andante non troppo e molto maestoso
  Mr. Walker and Conservatory Orchestra

Class of 1941 — Bachelor of Music Degree

Donald LeRoy Bartleman   St. James, Minnesota
  Major, Violin; minor, Piano
Philip Harbour Best   Helena, Arkansas
  Major, Piano; minor, History of Music
Arnold Samuel Blackburn   Ada, Oklahoma
  Major, Organ; minor, Piano
Melodia Louisa Blackmarr   Buffalo, New York
  Major, Piano and School Music

Recital program for Oberlin commencement, June 7, 1941

After Serkin's performance I went backstage to see him again. I told him that I wanted to apply for admission to the Curtis Institute of Music. Serkin was the most active member of a distinguished faculty there. No pianist at the Juilliard School of Music had a comparable concert reputation. Although I knew very little about the Curtis Institute, David Moyer, my piano teacher, was oblivious to its existence.

I wrote to request a catalog from the school. When I received the elegant white booklet with a cord parting the middle pages and a statement that its mission was to maintain the traditions of the past, I was convinced that Curtis would provide an ideal backdrop for the preparation of a concert career. The Josef Hofmann Prize mentioned in the booklet loomed like a magnet. But its only recipient was Jorge Bolet. When I graduated from Oberlin College in 1941 with the highest honors in my conservatory class, I was eager to find another challenging environment.

CURTIS INSTITUTE OF MUSIC

Auditions for admission to the Curtis Institute were held in the spring. I had about six weeks after my senior recital to concentrate on the required solo repertoire. My father wrote that he wanted to accompany me to the audition. He took the train from Washington, DC, to Philadelphia, where we met in Penn Station. It had been raining in Washington, DC, when he left. The weather was sunny in Philadelphia. He had his rubbers wrapped in a newspaper. We took a cab to the Curtis Institute. As we walked into the common room from the street, I was stunned to see the plush, deep red rug that covered the entire floor. I was allowed a warm-up period in one of the basement studios. My father sat quietly on a chair in the room while I practiced for twenty minutes.

The audition was held in a studio at the top of the stairs on the second floor. While waiting for my audition, I heard the Bach Prelude and Fugue in D Major from the first book of the *Well-Tempered Clavier* twice before I was ushered into the studio. Seated at a long table were Rudolf Serkin, Jorge Bolet, and Mme. Isabelle Vengerova. I played the same Bach that I had heard earlier, the first movement of the Waldstein Sonata of Beethoven, the Chopin Nocturne in D-flat, and the Octave Étude, op. 25, of Chopin. I had chosen and prepared all of these works without the help or advice of David Moyer.

After the audition, as my father and I were about to leave the building, I was asked to go to the second-floor office of the treasurer of the school. Mr. Mathis greeted us as we approached him in his office and told me that Mr. Serkin had accepted me for the next year as his student. When my father and I parted at Penn Station, I was sure that he felt the same sense of satisfaction that I experienced in achieving the goal that I had set. His slight parting smile conveyed more than any words that he could have spoken.

October 1 was the official opening date in 1941 for the beginning of my pursuit of an artist diploma from the Curtis Institute of Music. I arrived by train from Washington, DC, to Penn Station in Philadelphia and elected to walk to the school to save the taxi fare. From a half block away I could see several students, boys and girls, standing outside of the entrance to the building. I introduced myself to them. Some of them were Serkin students. I listened to their banter about their summer for a few minutes. Then we went inside to continue the conversation.

One short, pudgy boy said that he wanted to play the Beethoven Fourth Piano Concerto that he had learned if we could find a room with two pianos. We went up to the second floor of the annex. When no one volunteered to play with him, I said that I would, since I had studied the concerto at Oberlin. The boy was Eugene Istomin. To find myself surrounded by students younger than I was for the first time in my scholastic life was a bit odd. Istomin was two and a half years younger. I was eighteen when I graduated from Oberlin College, where I had grown from being five feet, four and a half to over six feet tall.

A few days after classes had begun at Curtis my new, beautiful green topcoat was stolen from the lobby of the common room. Green had become my favorite color. I was inwardly distraught. Mrs. Lockhart, who was in charge of the cafeteria that offered lunch in the annex, took me to a men's clothing store. (Sandwiches in the cafeteria were plump, delicious, and too expensive for my pocketbook.) She had been instructed to replace my topcoat. I chose a gray gabardine coat that was nicely styled. But I never became emotionally attached to it.

In my first meeting with Serkin at Curtis, he asked me to prepare for my lesson the following week the Bach Prelude and Fugue in B Minor from book 1 of the *Well-Tempered Clavier*, the Les Adieux Sonata of Beethoven, and three Chopin études: C-sharp minor, op. 10; F minor; and D-flat major, op. 25. As an admonition he added, "Read through the music carefully, find the tempo, and play in time."

The Curtis Institute had found a room for me about six blocks south of the school on Delancey Street. The home was occupied by a middle-aged black couple and a curmudgeonly father-in-law. It was located directly across from an active horse stable. A Steinway L grand piano was sent to the home and placed in a small room. I was instructed by the elderly handicapped man on how to light the gas stove on cold mornings—something that I did with trepidation each time. He firmly insisted that I perform my morning ablutions before 7:30 a.m. That was the precise time that he went to the bathroom.

About thirty years later, I met James Lewis, a professor in the Art Department of Morgan State College in Baltimore, Maryland. He told me that he had lived in the same room that I had occupied in the house on Delancey Street when he was a student at the University of Pennsylvania. The couple who owned the house showed him a painting that they had in their possession. He identified it as the work of Mary Cassatt, a famous American painter whose canvases have sold for as much as $2.5 million. Research confirmed that it was indeed an authentic product from her hand.

I cultivated the habit of listening to all of the Sunday broadcasts of the New York Philharmonic and the Saturday broadcasts of the NBC Symphony under Toscanini on my small portable radio. I heard Schnabel stop in a Mozart piano concerto, Toscanini falter in Wagner's Liebestod, and Rubinstein interrupted with the announcement of the Japanese attack on Pearl Harbor. When I learned that the Philadelphia Free Library had a huge collection of records, I would walk a mile and a quarter each week to listen to works that I was unfamiliar with.

Lessons with Serkin

I had memorized all of the assigned works for my first lesson. It was given in the large studio where the auditions were held. Two Steinway B pianos without the accelerated action patented by Josef Hofmann were in the carpeted, acoustically dead room. The large windows gave a view of the park in Rittenhouse Square. After greeting me, Serkin sat hunched over, palm under his chin and eyes closed, in an armchair ten feet from the piano (with its lid down) farthest from him to listen to my playing. He never looked at a score.

His first comments after I finished playing were about legato in the Bach prelude—more overlapping of the notes. In the sequential pattern of half steps in the Bach fugue, he stressed placing more weight on the first of the two notes. After hearing me play the first movement of Les Adieux, Serkin wanted a diminuendo in the descending horn motive (Lebewohl) with which the sonata begins. (In not observing this in his recording of this sonata, the poignancy created by this diminuendo is missing.) He pointed out the "tenuto" placed over the first inversion A-flat major chord that begins the exposition of the sonata after the introductory measures. ("Tenuto" means that a note should be held its full value, but no longer than that. His observation implied that the chord should be held longer. He would sometimes extend the duration of a chord beyond its notated value in his playing of other music.)

In the C-sharp-minor Chopin étude, he spoke about the subito "p" occurring after the five-note opening motive. This is possible to execute, but difficult to hear if the initial tempo is maintained. Observing the crescendo that follows is de rigueur. But it produces little dynamic change in the right-hand figuration. Most pianists ignore these markings as they crudely barrel through this étude. Serkin wanted the F-minor and D-flat-major études more legato. Tempos in my lessons were not issues that were discussed.

I repeated the same works for him in my second lesson. To my surprise, Jorge Bolet sat in on the lesson. I never understood why he was present nor did I ask him about it years later. This time, Serkin found that the F-minor étude was too legato. He complained that my "forte" was not loud enough. This became a recurring source of irritation for me. When I informed him toward the end of the year that I had already broken thirteen strings on my piano, he said nothing, nor did he offered any suggestions for or an explanation of this aberration.

My lessons were like concert performances. Every work was played in its entirety without any interruption from Serkin. There were no conversational exchanges during the lesson. Although I could have initiated some discussion by asking questions after I played, my focus was on conveying my preparation and comprehension of the music. I had to prove my ability in every lesson. There was never any question about my capacity to produce anything that he wanted.

Sometimes, Serkin said nothing about my playing. Occasionally he would make cautionary remarks like "Play close to the keys" that were unnecessary and irrelevant. Pedalling and ornamentation were never mentioned to me. Since I didn't have any technical problems that needed to be addressed, he had no reason to talk about this aspect of my development. Although he recognized the individuality of my playing in speaking to me about its "color" and "risk taking," he never discussed my future in terms of competitions or management opportunities. Perhaps I expected more from him as a person than he could give as a teacher. Without music, he was like a fish out of water.

In subsequent years his recitals became problematic for me because of the distracting physical movements, the aggressive dynamics (he didn't seem to care that an accent in "p" should be less than an accent in "f"), and the uncontrolled accents punctuating melodic lines that he was seemingly unaware of. In his efforts to project the music, intimacy and color were too often sacrificed for the projection of a big sonority. In playing duo recitals with Adolph Busch he was more restrained. Their recordings, however, reveal the lack of fidelity to the dynamic markings in the score. The thin, vibrato-impoverished sound of Busch's violin playing inevitably diverted one's attention to the piano part.

The next Beethoven sonata that I was assigned was op. 101. Serkin pounded the dotted rhythms of the march movement on the flat portion of the piano rack. (Gieseking played them like triplets.) Other exhortations were directed toward maintaining the propulsive energy in the fourth movement. After playing the last movement for him twice, I was given a week to solidify the sonata for a performance on one of the rare student concerts in Casimir Hall. All of the piano faculty, Mrs. Mary Curtis Bok, and Mr. Efrem Zimbalist were seated in the railed box area overlooking the students seated below in the hall. With that performance of the Beethoven Sonata op. 101, I was acknowledged to be the best pianist at Curtis.

Following the Sonata op. 101 of Beethoven, I learned the op. 110. Serkin found it hard to believe that I had not studied it before. Over the summer I learned the Chopin Sonata in B Minor, op. 58. In my second appearance on a student recital, my performance of it was even more enthusiastically received by everyone, including Mr. Zimbalist and Mrs. Bok.

Composition Lessons

A few weeks after I began my piano studies with Serkin, I talked with one of the composition students at Curtis in the common room. He told me about his lessons with Rosario Scalero. I liked the idea of working on counterpoint even though this could hardly be considered composition. I had begun to realize that I had a lot of unexpended energy after practicing five hours a day. At Oberlin I had been involved in many activities.

I spoke to Jane Hill, the indispensable and caring registrar, about my interest in taking composition lessons. She consulted with Scalero. He agreed to consider my submission of two works despite the fact that this could result in a belated admission to his class. I chose the song with the Paul Laurence Dunbar text and the "Danse Exotique" that I had composed at Oberlin. I was delighted to be accepted by Scalero. The combination of piano and composition provided the balance of musical activity that I needed.

All of Scalero's students, regardless of their previous accomplishments, began by working with six or seven *canti firmi*, creating counterpoint above and below them. Beginning with note against note in two-part eighteenth-century species counterpoint, they progressed into five-part writing before harmony was studied. After harmony came the writing of motets, chorale preludes, variations using models, and finally, as a graduation work, a sonata. This course was designed to cover three years of intensive study.

No text was used. Each student had a private lesson for an hour a week. Scalero's familiarity with all of the good solutions to his contrapuntal exercises reduced the examination and correction, if necessary, of the exercises to about fifteen minutes for my work. It was essential to write as many exercises that were both musically well shaped and technically perfect as possible. If Scalero was satisfied with the assignment, he would write out an example of the next species to be studied without any explanation being offered. If there were too many technical errors, the assignment was repeated; this happened to me only one time in three years after a misunderstanding.

Since I had taken counterpoint, canon, and fugue at Oberlin, none of these studies was challenging. I found that I had a particular gift for counterpoint and for conceiving melodic lines in my head. The weeks devoted to the study of harmony after the contrapuntal studies had been completed were less rigorously taught by Scalero. Toward the end of my study with him, I had a brief conversation with his young brother-in-law, Clermont Pepin, who was also a composition student. Scalero told Pepin that I had written "the best damn canons of any of his students."

My graduation work was a sonata for violin and piano. I worked on it in the summer of 1943. The usual busyness that was constant in our home prompted me to take my pencil and manuscript paper outside, where I sat in my father's car that was parked in front of our house. I was pleased that the beginning of the second movement that I wrote on the backseat was quite satisfactory when I tested it on the piano an hour later.

Scalero suggested that I "make a good copy" of the sonata and submit it to the Bearns Prize Committee at Columbia University in 1944. It didn't receive the award. But it was premiered at the Art Alliance in Philadelphia and made a strong impression. I played the piano part with Marie Shefeluk, who was the violinist in a trio that we had formed. Vincent Persichetti, a Philadelphia composer who taught for many years at Juilliard, was in the audience. He was intrigued by the sonata when we conversed about it after the performance. A few years later I withdrew the sonata from my limited list of compositions.

Scalero's bearing was patriarchal and self-important. A heavy Italian accent made his speech difficult to understand. After he had finished the instructional segment of the hour-long composition lesson, he would launch into a monologue about the state of contemporary music or recall past experiences with his music or that of his former students. Curling his white, waxed handlebar moustache with his right hand, he stated that Toscanini pointed out that the use of a trombone in certain measures in a work of Scalero was inadvisable. Scalero asserted that in the performance of the score, the trombone sounded just fine.

He was critical of "the dirty chords" in Menotti's music and ridiculed Stravinsky, whom he described as "destructive." Rachmaninoff was "the best of the second-rate composers." Ned Rorem, who studied counterpoint with Scalero for a year, was not viewed as sufficiently respectful in greeting him with a "Hi" before a lesson. Scalero affirmed that Sibelius marked the end of the era of great composers.

One of my lessons with Scalero was in his well-furnished apartment in Philadelphia. After he had seen my work, he began his predictable monologue. This speech was different, however, from any previous ones. He was planning to marry the sister of his pupil, Clermont Pepin. To dispel any thought that his fiancée would find greater satisfaction from a younger man, he exclaimed that he was "a virile man" (at age seventy-four).

Scalero also taught a class in music history. He read from his copious notes in lecture style as he sat behind his desk. The material that he presented on early music was more instructive than that found in the mediocre music history text (*History of Music* by Dickinson) that was used at Oberlin.

In one of my lessons, Scalero stated that the first intermezzo of op. 119 of Brahms anticipated Debussy. Scalero was a pupil of Mandyczewski, who had edited the complete works of Brahms. In a letter to Clara Schumann, Brahms described this character piece as "dissonant" and full of melancholy. A contemporary observation made by an unidentified theorist describes the intermezzo as "Schonbergian," lacking in tonality.

None of these statements makes sense. The first measure can be analyzed as harmonies that extend the triadic components of common practice music to elevenths and thirteenths. It is unlikely that Debussy would write a series of descending intervals in the manner of Brahms. It is amusing to read that Brahms found his compilation of thirds as "regretfully dissonant."

Curtis Predecessor

Preceding me at Curtis was Muriel Smith, an attractive black mezzo-soprano. I would visit her occasionally in the evening after dinner to play the accompaniments of lieder that she knew. She found it difficult to study anything that did not relate to singing. She would prod me into doing her counterpoint lessons for her theory class with the caveat that there should be some mistakes left in the exercises. Her charm was such that the radiance of her smile and her natural effusiveness could efface any inclination of Frau Shumway, the German instructor, to complain about her tardiness in arriving ten minutes after the class had begun. Muriel left Curtis before I graduated to share the role of Carmen in the Broadway production of *Carmen Jones*. After considerable success in London, she abandoned her singing and acting career to join a cult, Moral Rearmament. When she returned to the United States, she worked as a secretary at Virginia State University until her death.

Summer at Oberlin 1942

At the end of my first year at Curtis, my mother was concerned that I had not obtained a master's degree in music. Since Oberlin offered that degree, I applied for admission into the graduate program. I planned to complete the degree in piano in two summers after being at Curtis for the academic year. My former teacher, David Moyer, was available for the first part of the summer of 1942. I had no choice in the selection of another piano teacher for the second half. The only teacher available was John Elvin with whom my sister, Frances, had studied.

My lessons with Elvin confirmed what Frances had told me about him. He talked incessantly for half of the allocated time. During the remaining time he had nothing to tell me after I finally got a chance to play. I had a list of works from Serkin to prepare for the next year. Elvin tried to dissuade me from learning the *Kreisleriana* of Schumann. It was obvious that he didn't know the work. One would have thought that as a graduate student I would have a choice in what I wanted to study. My lessons with him were a waste of time. I completed my language requirement, which was in French, but I didn't return to Oberlin the next summer to complete the master's degree.

When I was a junior at Oberlin, Poister, my organ teacher, introduced me to a German student, Ludwig Lenel, who had come to the college after the first semester had begun. Poister asked me to show Lenel the capabilities of the organ in Finney Chapel. When I returned to Oberlin to pursue a master's degree in 1942, Lenel had been given a teaching position in the conservatory that summer. Before emigrating to the United States he had received organ lessons from Dr. Albert Schweitzer. Schweitzer frequently stayed with Lenel's family when he was in Heidelberg, and Lenel became his godson. After living in Illinois and New York City, Lenel spent twenty-seven years as a professor of organ, a choir director, and composer at Muhlenberg College in Pennsylvania.

Second Year at Curtis

The Curtis Institute found another room for me when I returned to Philadelphia for my second year of study. It was located several blocks below Delancey Street in South Philadelphia. The room was on the third floor of the house. My Steinway L piano had to be hoisted outside of the building through the window because it was impossible to have it carried up two flights of steps. The lady who rented the room to me was very kind. Every week she made a huge pot of chicken soup. I had to partake of it if I was there at lunchtime. The amount of water used for the soup required more seasoning than she added to make it palatable. It was rather tasteless.

The beginning of my second year at Curtis (1942) was clouded by the prospect of my being inducted into the armed services. I had received a draft notice requiring me to appear at an army base outside of Washington, DC, in Virginia. There was the likelihood that my studies at Curtis would be curtailed for several years. Knowing this, Esther Aronauskaite, another Serkin student, in a wonderful gesture of friendship, collected enough money from other students to give me all of the available volumes of the *Oxford Edition of the Chopin Piano Works*.

Fortunately, I was rejected for service and classified "4-F." My poor parents were undoubtedly worried sick over the possibility of my being drafted. After my induction appearance, I returned the next day to Philadelphia to the amazement of my friends. The salvaged years made me even more determined to make the most of my experience at Curtis.

My mother had plans for me after I had completed my second year at Curtis. She thought that it was important that I have a government insurance policy. I obtained a summer job at the Pentagon for that purpose. The job was also intended to provide me with some personal income. To get to the Pentagon, a complex that was dedicated in 1943, I took a streetcar at 7:45 in the morning to downtown Washington, DC, and a bus to Arlington, Virginia, which is across the Potomac River that separates Washington from Virginia.

My job as a file clerk was to correct the misfiling of scores of yellow sheets, copies that had been placed inside rows of gray metal letter files. Several middle-aged women worked in the same room at different tasks. My work was unsupervised. I never became acquainted with the rest of the staff. Lunch offered in a large cafeteria provided some relief from the tedium of alphabetizing these papers. The best part of the job was the air-conditioned building.

After six weeks I told my mother that I had enough of this boring work. When I came home in the late afternoon after being in an air-conditioned building, the summer heat was even more unbearable. I found it difficult to practice at night to learn the repertoire that had been typed out for Serkin to give to me. This was far more important than any job. Besides, I had worked long enough to qualify for life insurance.

Music in Washington, DC

I spent my Christmas and Easter holidays at home. During this period there were free concerts given in the Library of Congress. Tickets had to be obtained from Kitts Music Store in Washington, DC, because the small hall had a limited capacity.

I often attended performances by the Budapest String Quartet, the most frequently heard ensemble for these concerts in the Coolidge Auditorium. Four Stradivari instruments, owned by the Library of Congress, were used. The Budapest String Quartet had become the best known string quartet in this country because of their many concert appearances and their recordings on Columbia Records. But Joseph Roisman, the first violinist, had intonation lapses that were disconcerting. The repertoire played was quite restricted—Haydn, Mozart, Beethoven, and Brahms.

George Szell, the conductor of the Cleveland Orchestra, was the guest pianist in the Mozart Piano Quartet in G Minor K. 478. on one program. He was obviously very nervous. In the final movement he led the Budapest String Quartet in a merry chase that got faster with each of his entrances. To call this a propulsive performance would be to de-emphasize the breathlessness of the result. I was invariably the only black person in the audience for these programs.

In one of the parks in Washington, DC, there were outdoor string quartet concerts in the summer. I heard the Primrose String Quartet, founded in 1939 by William Primrose, in a performance of the Smetana String Quartet *From My Life*. The viola part was clearly important in this group.

I was standing in line to obtain a ticket to hear David Oistrakh play the Beethoven Violin Concerto with a French orchestra in Paris in 1958. I noticed that Primrose was also in the line ahead of me. When I spoke to him, he invited me to have lunch with him in a cafe the next day. He spoke candidly about his experiences at Curtis.

After I had graduated from Curtis, he accepted a second black student in his viola class. (Romaine Brown, his first student, studied with Primrose for a year when I began my lessons with Serkin. Romaine was also a jazz pianist. He played several nights a week in a nightclub. I did not see him often at Curtis. But when I did, the most noticeable feature about him was his eyes. They looked like small yellow moons from his lack of sleep.)

Primrose had encouraged his black student to apply for a position in the Pittsburgh Symphony conducted by Fritz Reiner. The student failed to show up for the audition that had been arranged for him. This was very disappointing to Primrose, who was a generous and kind man, a great violist who had gone out of his way to promote integration in a major symphony orchestra.

A barge tethered to a dock on the Potomac River was the site of evening concerts by the National Symphony. The orchestra played on a deck with a large reflective shell behind them. The breeze from the water was refreshing on uncomfortably hot nights. Jose Iturbi and Jesus Sanroma were some of the piano soloists. I also heard Percy Grainger play the Grieg Piano Concerto. It was stated in a newspaper article that he walked hundreds of miles with a knapsack to many gigs.

When I would alert my mother to a Bell Telephone Hour that was featuring Heifetz or Toscanini conducting the NBC Orchestra, she would finish her chores in time for the entire family—my father, grandmother, and sister—to assemble upstairs in my parents' room to listen to the broadcast. After the program ended, little was said. But this concerted support of my interests was extraordinary.

My parents' bedroom was the warmest room in the house on cold winter nights. We often sat in the dark, watching the lights darting down the empty streets from passing cars, beams reflecting on the walls of the room, listening to my mother as she reminisced about whatever occurred to her at the moment.

More about Curtis

At the end of my third year at Curtis the Steinway L piano that was loaned to me was shipped to Washington, DC, for the entire summer without any cost to my parents. We still had a Chickering grand piano in the parlor. The Steinway was placed in the library, which was already rather small. The Schumann Piano Concerto was one of the works on the list that Serkin gave me to study. After I learned each movement of the concerto, my sister would play the second piano part on the Chickering in the parlor. I would strain to hear it in the library as the sound snaked around the hallway connecting the two rooms.

I heard that there was a move afoot at Curtis to create a student council. An election was held. I was among several who were voted to become members of the student group. We made an appointment to meet Efrem Zimbalist, the director, to request a record player and to have more student recitals. Mr. Zimbalist emphatically stated that he did not endorse the idea of listening to records. Nevertheless, a beautiful console was purchased and made available to the students. After the very first time that it was used, the record player was left on overnight. It wouldn't play the next day. Something had burned out. Our privilege to use it was rescinded. But we were granted the use of Casimir Hall for a few informal evening programs that were not attended by the faculty.

William Primrose conducted a chamber music class in which I was enrolled. The only ensemble at Curtis that gave public performances was a piano trio in which I played. The piece de resistance was the Archduke Trio of Beethoven. Our trio had two cellists, Shirley Trepel and Marion Davies, who alternated for the Beethoven. We played in several homes for senior citizens. I accompanied both of them in their graduation recitals. On one occasion when their lessons were given in Gregor Piatigorsky's apartment in the Warwick Hotel off of Rittenhouse Square, Mrs. Piatigorsky gave us fresh strawberries and cream—an uncommon treat for the middle of winter. Shirley became the principal cellist in the Houston Symphony. Marion was the principal cellist in the Dallas Symphony.

Serkin's visits to Curtis were essentially detours from a frenetic concert schedule. He taught three students during each visit. I received a lesson every week. It often stretched beyond an hour and sometimes beyond the natural light in the studio. The few reservations that I had about his teaching were never expressed. Other students were much more vociferous. Myra Ghitis, who occasionally had lessons with Serkin for two years, would tearfully tell me about the frustrations that she experienced in her lessons. She did not return to Curtis for a third year. My sister, Frances, who studied with Serkin for a year after her graduation from Oberlin, found him to be enigmatic. A young boy whom Serkin asked me to teach experienced a nervous breakdown after Serkin vetoed his return to Curtis for a second year. Ironically, Serkin was still the most genuinely complimentary teacher that I ever had. After I played the Chopin Ballade in F Minor for him, he remarked, "At your best, you are the equal of any pianist. The cream will always rise to the top." But he never lifted a finger to help me get there.

Serkin had a great deal of respect for Rachmaninoff. Esther Aronauskaite told me that during a lesson that she had with Serkin in New

York, Rachmaninoff telephoned him. Serkin became very excited before taking the call. In one of my lessons I played two of the Mendelssohn Songs without Words for Serkin. I told him that Rachmaninoff added a measure in his recording of the Spinning Song. Serkin retorted facetiously that "Rachmaninoff never looked at the music."

Serkin played a few of Rachmaninoff's preludes for him and gave one performance of the Second Piano Concerto with an orchestra in Canada. When I asked him about it, he tersely said, "Never again."

Serkin's relationship with Horowitz was quite different. There was an element of awe in his appreciation of Horowitz's ability to sight-read. Serkin told me to listen to the sound that he produced, but to avoid any imitation of him. He did not talk to me about any other pianists.

When Serkin brought Mieczyslaw Horszowski to Curtis as his assistant in my second year, I had a lesson with him if Serkin was unable to teach that week. Those lessons were the last of the day for Horszowski. I would ask him each time if I could join him for dinner at the Automat. He was a vegetarian.

I limited myself to a dollar a day for food—which meant that I never spent more than fifty cents for that meal. My father would certainly have given me more money if I asked for it. Since my sister had matriculated at Oberlin College the year after my graduation, I wanted to limit the support that he would find necessary to give me.

When I spoke to Horszowski about an imminent concert that Horowitz was giving in Carnegie Hall, I received a ticket from Wanda, Horowitz's wife, for that recital. Horszowski also showed Horowitz the three short piano pieces that I played on my debut recital in Town Hall. But I never asked him how they were received.

Horszowski seldom made any comments about my playing. He seemed to enjoy talking in his limited English about concerts that he had heard in New York or about evenings with Horowitz in the latter's apartment. Casals allegedly asserted that Horszowski could be testy, and I can attest that he could be sarcastic. I "shink" (think), as he would say, that he didn't want to contradict anything that Serkin might have said in my lessons with him.

Esther Aronauskaite was charmed by Horszowski because he could suggest fingerings for her small hand. She had come to the United States from Lithuania after having been in a concentration camp in World War II. Her health deteriorated after she succumbed to tuberculosis. Before

I finished my studies at Curtis, she had been placed in a sanitarium on the outskirts of Philadelphia. Her infectious love of Mozart sonatas and Chopin mazurkas still reverberates in my memory.

Gian-Carlo Menotti

Gian-Carlo Menotti taught orchestration. What little information was conveyed came as casual references to instrumental timbre. No textbook was used or suggested. There was no discussion about many of the instruments of the orchestra. Nothing was said about percussion, and there was only one assignment for the entire course.

For one particular class, Menotti brought in manuscripts of his piano concerto that he had shown to Horowitz. I was taken aback by all of the erasures on the pages. Menotti's remarks about his concerto were not related to orchestration. He talked about the anti-romantic texture of the music and the use of scalar figurations reminiscent in their sparseness to Scarlatti sonatas and Mozart concertos. He expressed some antipathy toward the Brahms Concerti.

For the final exam of the course, Menotti asked us to orchestrate a work that would be played for the entire class. I orchestrated a set of variations that I had composed for a lesson with my composition teacher, Rosario Scalero. They were based on the first of the Kinder-szenen of Robert Schumann. I arranged the variations for string quartet because I knew that some of my friends would be available to play them.

When I arrived at Curtis on the day of the exam, Jane Hill, the registrar, informed me that the class would meet in Casimir Hall instead of in Scalero's room. Entering the hall from the stage entrance, I was astonished to see Samuel Barber sitting with Menotti. When my variations were played, he clapped heartily, as he did for all of the works that were performed. This was the first time that any music of mine had been applauded. My knowledge of orchestration was derived from my own efforts in studying scores, listening to music, and reading all of the available publications on the subject.

Menotti also taught a course in opera. What we learned in it was mostly about his disenchantment with the Metropolitan Opera. He railed against it ad nauseum. He favored young singers in his operas. There was no discussion of any opera. He winged it for every class.

Mrs. Bok financed performances of Menotti's one-act opera *The Old Maid and the Thief*, which was done in the Academy of Music in Philadelphia. This work is essentially fluff. The opera class received tickets to see *The Medium* in New York. It was the first opera to be premiered as a Broadway production. *The Consul*, which I saw in Washington, DC, with a different cast, was quite moving.

Curtis Recitals

The faculty recitals at Curtis were welcomed with great anticipation, but were generally not inspiring. Horszowski never played louder than a mezzo forte. His performance of several Mozart piano sonatas on one program was prosaic, lacking in sparkle and imagination. A rare appearance by Efrem Zimbalist was uninvolving because of his preference for a pure, white tone. Primrose's recital exhibited much macho without any semblance of inwardness. The performance by Serkin of the Bach Toccata in E Minor was beautifully contoured, the best performance on his program. Salzedo included several of his compositions on a recital. One of them, entitled *Felines*, evoked one suppressed snicker after another until the entire audience was suffocating from the plaintive suggestions of a cat in labor.

Each student at Curtis was allowed two tickets a year to attend a Philadelphia Orchestra performance. Sometimes Jane Hill, the registrar, would offer additional concert tickets if they were available. This special dispensation allowed me to hear a Heifetz recital in the Academy of Music from the Curtis box in the balcony close to the stage. The highly audible scratching in his playing of a solo Bach partita that began the program was both distracting and musically disturbing.

I went backstage with a pupil of Efrem Zimbalist. We watched Heifetz as he wiped the resin from his Guarneri with loving care. His recitals always seemed unbalanced and a little condescending with the entire second half of the program consisting of lightweight works. This arrangement was undoubtedly advantageous for the endless touring that he did.

A few years later I heard Heifetz play in Carnegie Hall. The principal work on the program was the Strauss Violin Sonata, which he slashed through without any demonstrable interest in elevating this work to a more appreciable plane. His accompanist was, as usual, left to finger his part as unobtrusively as possible. Another disappointing, but well-hyped concert. The recordings and videos of Heifetz clearly show him at his best.

Philadelphia's Problem

Curtis was a wonderful oasis in the midst of a city besmirched by segregation. Restaurants located within blocks of the school were blatantly discriminatory. On one occasion when I was with friends, we stood in line for a table for over forty-five minutes and left after being convinced that we would not be seated. Others who had arrived after us were escorted to tables.

In another incident, an attendant in a self-service cafeteria popular with Curtis students approached me as I was filling my plate behind two friends. It was lunchtime and we had just finished rehearsing the Brahms Horn Trio. He demanded that I leave the restaurant. I ignored him, paid my bill, and sat with my friends.

Perhaps the most egregious episode occurred at the entrance of the First Baptist Church at Seventeenth and Samson Street. The choir and organist of this church had a good reputation. I decided to attend its morning service. As I approached, the usher standing at the door said, "Why don't you go to your own church?" I walked past him and sat down on a pew in the back of the church.

Graduation

Although I could have received my artist diploma in piano in 1944, I decided to spend another year with Serkin to work on repertoire. The following year I shared (as was customary then) my graduation recital with Pierrette Alarie, a Canadian soprano. Pierrette had graciously learned two of my songs, which she sang on a recital at Lincoln University, a black college in Pennsylvania. I accompanied her for that program.

My segment of the graduation recital began with the Liszt Piano Sonata in B Minor. After the concert, Efrem Zimbalist told my parents—who had come up from Washington, DC, with my former piano teacher, Lillian Mitchell—that "there has never been a better student at the Curtis Institute." Pierrette won the Metropolitan Opera Auditions and made her debut with the Metropolitan Opera Company in 1945.

In the spring of 1945 Serkin told me that Efrem Zimbalist "wanted to do something for me." I was not sure what this implied. My father had already determined that it would be important for me to make my New York recital debut. A few suspenseful weeks passed before I learned that Mr. and Mrs. Zimbalist wanted to present me in a Town Hall debut recital. Arrangements were made with the National Concert Artists for a photo session in New York for posters and the concert program. I heard nothing more from Serkin, who did not even discuss a choice of works with me for the concert. Neither did he offer any excuse or apology for not being able to attend the November 13th recital.

LEVENTRITT COMPETITION

In September of 1945, about two months before my scheduled Town Hall debut, I entered the Leventritt Competition in New York. For the first round of the auditions, pianists were required to play a movement from a concerto of their choice and a solo piano work. Just before I was to play, Arthur Balsam, who provided the second piano accompaniments for the contestants, spoke to me. He had never played the Third Piano Concerto of Rachmaninoff. We spoke about the opening tempo. He sight-read his part perfectly in the audition.

The following day, the Leventritt Competition posted the names of the pianists who would be playing in the next round. Serkin and Adolf Busch were the judges. I was incredulous when my name was not listed. I called Serkin to ask him if this was a mistake. The answer that he gave me was inexplicable. He had expected that my playing would have been more brilliant. (Anyone familiar with this score would not be able to judge its virtuosic potential after listening to only eight pages. Moreover, I had studied the concerto with him.) But he also stated that Adolf Busch, who was the other judge, said that "he had never heard the Schubert Moment Musical played more beautifully." I knew that I could not have played both works better.

Marcel Tabuteau, the principal oboist of the Philadelphia Orchestra, made a similar comment to his student, Laila Storck, about my playing of the beginning of the Rachmaninoff Piano Concerto no. 3 when I made my orchestral debut.

It would have been inconceivable for anyone to have foreseen that I would be inducted into the American Classical Music Hall of Fame in 2000 with my former teacher, Rudolf Serkin.

NOVEMBER 1945

The centerpiece of my Town Hall recital on November 13, 1945, was the *Kreisleriana* of Schumann. This was the work that I had planned to play for Horowitz when Serkin invited him to hear three of his students at Curtis. (Horowitz predictably cancelled his visit at the last minute.) Walking out on the stage of Town Hall, I was surprised to see that the hall was three-quarters full. I had only been to New York a few times and my parents had no connections there.

GEORGE WALKER, the 23-year-old American pianist who gives his first New York recital on Tuesday evening, November 13, was born in Washington, D. C., of West Indian parentage.

Upon completing his course at the Oberlin Conservatory of Music he continued his piano studies at the Curtis Institute of Music in Philadelphia, under Rudolph Serkin and Mieczyslaw Horszowski, and composition with Rosario Scalero, graduating in 1945.

Mr. Walker will include in his program a group of recently completed works of his own, "Three Pieces for Piano," which will have their premiere performance at this recital.

Program

I
Prelude and Fugue in C sharp major . . . . BACH
    (from Well Tempered Clavichord, Vol. II)

Sonata, op. 101 . . . . BEETHOVEN

II
Kreisleriana, op. 16 . . . . SCHUMANN
    Ausserst bewegt
    Sehr innig und nicht zu rasch
    Sehr aufgeregt
    Sehr langsam
    Sehr lebhaft
    Sehr langsam
    Sehr rasch
    Schnell und spielend

INTERMISSION

III
Three Pieces . . . . GEORGE WALKER
            (first performance in New York)

Barcarolle
Four Etudes
    C sharp minor, op. 10
    G flat major, op. 10 } . . . . CHOPIN
    C flat minor, op. 10
    B minor, op. 25

IV
Toccata, op. 11 . . . . PROKOFIEFF

Steinway Piano

Tickets: $2.40, $1.80, $1.20 and 90¢. Loges, seating six, $18. Tax included.

Management: NATIONAL CONCERT AND ARTISTS CORPORATION
ALFRED H. MORTON, *President*   •   MARKS LEVINE, *Director, Concert Division*
711 FIFTH AVENUE, NEW YORK 22, N. Y.

Program for my first Town Hall recital, November 13, 1945

My mother, I was told, became upset when the stagehand brought out a second piano bench after I played the Bach Prelude and Fugue in C-sharp Major bk. 2 to begin the recital and a third bench after the conclusion of the Beethoven Sonata op. 101. In the rehearsal for the recital the previous day I had marked the bench that I intended to use with chalk. The same stagehand who was hired for this concert had made not one, but two unnerving mistakes.

After playing my fourth encore, I walked backstage where Dean Dixon, the black conductor who had conducted Toscanini's NBC Orchestra, was waiting. He introduced himself and said that "he wanted to be the first to congratulate me." I was also delighted to meet some of my father's relatives who came for the concert.

George Walker, Town Hall debut, 1941

Josephine Brown was the first relative of my father whom we had met in Washington, DC. She came from Cuba to spend a few weeks in our home before settling in New York City. She was quite lovely, with a beautiful complexion and a delightfully animated persona. Never having seen snow in Cuba, she was completely enthralled by the first snowflakes of the winter that wafted outside the large window in our parlor. Her son, Georg Stanford Brown, was a scholastic delinquent who became interested in acting. Moving back to California after studying in the American Musical and Dramatic Academy in New York, he starred in the television police series *The Rookies*. I met him years later in Washington, DC, at a reception at the White House during the disastrous Reagan administration. He introduced me to his wife, Tyne Daly, the actress.

Most incredible of all was the invitation extended to my entire family by a West Indian family whom I did not know. Dr. and Mrs. Carroll requested that we come to their home for a reception. The press releases from the National Concert Artists Management announcing that a West Indian pianist would be playing a concert of classical music in Town Hall had electrified the community of highly successful immigrants from the Caribbean who resided in Harlem. (Dean Dixon's mother was born in the West Indies.) The imposing brownstone home of Dr. and Mrs. Carroll on 144th Street was crammed with prosperous physicians and dentists. Also present was a businessman who owned eighty-five taxicabs, all of which he said that he personally inspected periodically.

None of the three daughters of the Carrolls appeared to have any musical talent. But Vinnette, the oldest daughter, became a prominent theater producer and the first black woman director of a Broadway musical. There is a theater named after her in Fort Lauderdale, Florida.

The review of my Town Hall recital that appeared in the *New York Times* began, "A notable debut recital . . . an authentic talent of marked individuality and fine musical insight . . . a rare combination of elegance and sincerity . . . an unusual technique . . . a technical competence and a sensitivity rarely heard at debut recitals."

I could only savor this success briefly. In two weeks I was scheduled to make my orchestral debut with the Philadelphia Orchestra. In the spring of 1945 I had entered the Philadelphia Youth Auditions Competition to have the opportunity of playing a concerto with the Philadelphia Orchestra. I had learned the third concerto of Rachmaninoff the previous summer. It was not a work on the repertoire list

PIANO RECITAL GIVEN BY GEORGE WALKER

New York Times, Nov. 14, 1945

A notable debut recital was given last night at Town Hall by George Walker, young Washington, D. C., pianist of West Indian parentage, who has been a pupil of Rudolph Serkin and Mieczyslaw Horszowski. In a program ranging from Bach and Beethoven through Schumann and Chopin to Prokofieff, and including three three small pieces of his own, Mr. Walker revealed an authentic talent of marked individuality and fine musical insight. He disclosed a rare combination of elegance and sincerity, an unusual technique and a nice basic tone, with lovely coloring.

The Beethoven A-major Sonata, Opus 101, was played with an understanding not often found in a young pianist, and the Kreisleriana of Schumann was a model of quiet, introspective music-making, with the true Schumann richness of feeling, notably in No. 6, B-flat major, "sehr langsam." The next, "sehr rasch," in C minor and E-flat major, gave the player an opportunity to display his technical brilliancy, as did four études of Chopin, three from the first book, C-sharp minor, G-flat major and C-flat minor, and one, B minor from the second.

The Chopin Barcarolle, a touchstone of any pianist's quality, was played with an understanding, a technical competence and a sensitiveness rarely heard at debut recitals. The performance of the closing Prokofieff Toccata, Opus 11, was suitably dashing and intelligent in its delineation of the ideas.

Mr. Walker's own three pieces, performed here for the first time, while slight and lacking in originality, were well composed and showed promise.   R. L.

New York Times *review of recital debut*

that Serkin gave me to study over the summer. But I had played it for him twice. The climactic beauty of this concerto was far more exciting to me than the more familiar Piano Concerto no. 2. For the audition, I played part of the first movement of the Piano Concerto no. 3 for a jury of two persons, Eugene Ormandy and William Kapell.

I had heard interesting details about Kapell from Esther Aronauskaite. She met him at a summer resort and recalled his compulsive practicing and the nervous tension that caused pimples on his face. Kapell's success in performing the Khatchaturian Piano Concerto sparked a burgeoning career. A few weeks after the audition, I received a letter informing me that I had been chosen to play with the Philadelphia Orchestra in November of 1945.

I had only one rehearsal of the Rachmaninoff Piano Concerto no. 3 at 10:00 a.m. on the morning of the concert. Ormandy led the Philadelphia Orchestra past numerous mistakes from some of the players from the beginning of the work to the end without stopping. It was obvious that the orchestra had not played the accompaniment in several years. I played the entire score without the cuts taken in all of the recorded performances by Rachmaninoff and Horowitz.

The Academy of Music was filled to the rafters for the evening concert. Backstage was Gregor Piatigorsky, who was also playing on the program. Inexplicably, Ormandy slowed the tempo that he took in the rehearsal for the final pages. I had to make an adjustment for his mistake. The audience response to the performance was wildly enthusiastic and heartwarming. A review in a Philadelphia newspaper described the applause as "thunderous."

POSTGRADUATE STUDY AT CURTIS

Prior to my orchestral debut with the Philadelphia Orchestra in November 1945, I had asked Mr. Zimbalist, the director of the Curtis Institute, if I could continue my composition studies with Rosario Scalero. He granted my request. I was pleased to be permitted to do so because I wanted to compose a string quartet with some supervision. But the lessons that I had with Scalero as a postgraduate student were quite perfunctory. He had nothing to say about what I showed him other than to suggest at my first lesson that I pick a model and follow it. He didn't seem capable of working with a student on anything that was beyond the material that he used for undergraduate studies.

I was now living for the second consecutive year in West Philadelphia. Muriel Smith had suggested that I contact her Aunt Henny (Miss Henrietta Lopez) when I was unable to find a satisfactory place in South Philadelphia. (I was obliged to relinquish my room in South Philadelphia when I went to Washington, DC, for the summer.) She was a small, cheerful lady who owned a small home that was two blocks from the end of the line of the El (Elevated Train) that carried passengers into the center of Philadelphia. There was also an Automat a few blocks from her home.

Occasionally, I would meet a high school friend, George Butcher, who was working on his doctorate in mathematics at the University of Pennsylvania. George told me about the dinners, with dessert included, at Father Divine's Church for twenty-five cents. The portions of black southern fare were huge. Father Divine was a deified figure in South Philadelphia who had convinced his followers that he was immortal, until he died.

In the room where my Steinway piano had been installed was a bookcase containing about twenty-five red-leather-bound books of the Harvard Classics, a great book series that began with the Greek philosophers. I was able to compose and practice the entire day in solitude until Miss Lopez returned from work. I made a habit of reading a portion of a book from her library many evenings before going to bed.

Miss Lopez's kitchen was always stacked with newspapers that she never disposed of when she had finished reading them. After I had moved to New York, I was greatly saddened to learn that she had perished in a fire that may have begun on her first floor. She would sometimes offer me vanilla custard in the evening.

At Curtis I had elected to take an Italian language course and a class on the Renaissance from Dr. Domenico Vittorini, a professor at the University of Pennsylvania. I had begun learning about antiquity in dissecting Cicero in my first high school Latin class. Dr. Vittorini was a warm, patient teacher who spoke with a genuine love of the humanists in the Renaissance. He liked to take issue with perceived inaccuracies in the writings of other scholars of the period—John Addington Symonds, Bernard Berenson, and other historians. When I began to teach, I found that I also liked to discover errors that constitute a misrepresentation of facts. Vittorini's discussions of Dante, Erasmus, and Machiavelli were vigorous and discerning. I would not have composed my *Overture: In Praise of Folly* had I not read the satirical encomium "The Praise of Folly," by the Dutch scholar Erasmus.

While living in West Philadelphia, I became acquainted with the soprano Camilla Williams. Her career developed after winning a Marian Anderson Fellowship. An emotional audition effected a contract with Columbia Artists Management. I would occasionally practice with her.

Camilla asked me to accompany her in an appearance at a one-hundred-dollar-a-plate dinner event. We did not rehearse in the spacious room before the guests arrived. The piano on the stage was a small white grand. I was not aware until I sat down on the bench to play that the pedal mechanism was missing. I immediately recalled that Robert Casadesus had allegedly stated that Mozart did not require much pedal. Unfortunately, there was no Mozart in Camilla's selection of songs. Legato playing had never been made more necessary. Shortly after that mishap, she became the first black singer to receive a contract from a major American opera company, the New York City Center Opera.

ORIGIN OF THE *LYRIC FOR STRINGS*

When I finished the first movement of my string quartet, I began to compose a contrasting slow movement. Scalero had mentioned in one of his monologues that Barber's Adagio for Strings was influenced by his study of the slow movement of the String Quartet op. 135 of Beethoven. This string quartet from his last period was one of my favorite chamber music works. In studying the score again, I found no connection between the slow, spiraling line of the Barber adagio and the sectional structure of the slow movement of the Beethoven work. Toscanini had made a string orchestra arrangement of the second movement of the op. 135 string quartet.

When I was at Oberlin, I would write to my parents every week. My mother would respond immediately after receiving my letter. Miss Lopez did not have a telephone in her house. When I would call home to talk to my parents, I had to use a public phone. Using a phone in a telephone booth, I called my father one afternoon to ask him how things were there. I was shocked to learn from him that my grandmother had just died.

I took the train to Washington, DC, the next day in order to attend her funeral. Walking behind the casket with my father as we passed through the portal of the sanctuary of our church en route to the cemetery, I glanced at my father. A single tear hovered just beneath his left eyelid.

Shortly after I completed the three movements of my string quartet, Seymour Lipkin, who had auditioned to study with Serkin the same year that I did, told me that he was going to conduct a string orchestra comprised of Curtis students on a series of radio programs sponsored by a Philadelphia bank. He asked me to play a four-hand work of Schubert with him on one of the programs. I suggested to him that I could make a string orchestra arrangement of the second movement of my string quartet if he would conduct it on another program. When I made the arrangement, he gave the first performance of the movement on the radio. It was called Lament for String Orchestra.

The following winter, Richard Bales gave the first public performance of it during his annual American Music Festival in the Mellon Art Gallery (now the National Gallery of Art) in Washington, DC. I changed the title of the slow movement for that performance to Adagio for String Orchestra. Finding that title too prosaic and unoriginal, I decided that for subsequent performances, *Lyric for Strings* more aptly described the character of the work. It was dedicated to my recently deceased grandmother, Malvina King.

It occurred to me to show the score of my *Lyric* to Eugene Ormandy since I had played the Rachmaninoff Piano Concerto no. 3 with him five months earlier. My plan was to arrive at the Academy of Music at the conclusion of an orchestra rehearsal. This appeared to be a workable tactic. But after Ormandy had walked off of the stage at the end of the rehearsal, it took me some time to get backstage. I saw his diminutive figure and shiny bald head as he was ascending an iron staircase going up from the stage. I rushed to speak to him and said, "Mr. Ormandy, may I talk with you?" Looking sideways toward me, without pausing, he said, "I'm very busy." After a few more steps he disappeared when he reached the next level.

After completing my first string quartet, I enlisted four students to play the entire work on a recital at Curtis. The first violinist for that concert was Nathan Goldstein. Several weeks later, the Curtis Institute was invited to present a chamber music concert at the Juilliard School of Music. My string quartet was included on that program. Aaron Rosand replaced Goldstein as the first violinist. Rosand, whose teacher was Efrem Zimbalist, eventually became the head of the violin department at Curtis. Karen Tuttle, the violist in both performances, taught at Curtis for an extended period before retiring.

In the original version of the first movement there was a difficult viola solo. (In the revised edition those measures were divided between the second violin and the viola.) When my string quartet was played for Primrose in a chamber music class, Karen's discomfort with the solo in the development section of the first movement was evident. Primrose snatched the viola from her and sight-read the passage perfectly—with élan. Earlier, he had been complaining that no one knew how to sight-read.

SPECIAL EVENTS

After the conclusion of the Juilliard concert, I was pleasantly surprised to meet a black woman who introduced herself to me. Her name was Perdita Duncan. She succeeded Nora Holt as the music critic for the *Amsterdam News*, a black newspaper in New York. When I told Ms. Duncan that I lived in Philadelphia, she suggested that I get in touch with her whenever I was in New York. After I moved to St. Albans, New York, I contacted her and became her unpaid assistant, covering a few concerts and movies using a press pass and writing reviews of them for her.

The most unusual event that I attended was a luncheon at the Jewish Theological Seminary on Broadway in New York. The guest speaker was Dr. Harry Emerson Fosdick, the first pastor of the Riverside Church established by John D. Rockefeller Jr. Fosdick began his talk by speaking about how he became a minister. He recalled walking into a room filled with students at his college, Colgate University. When he saw a young woman in the crowded room, he knew immediately that she was his soul mate for life. Theirs was a storybook marriage. Fosdick was considered to be an outspoken opponent of racism and injustice. He began his outstanding career as the pastor of the First Baptist Church in Montclair, New Jersey.

BALTIMORE CONCERTS

I learned the Piano Concerto no. 2 of Brahms in the summer of 1946 after returning to Washington, DC, to live with my parents. I was engaged to play it with the Baltimore Symphony in the winter of 1947. Since I had never rehearsed the concerto with another pianist playing the second piano part, my former piano teacher, Mrs. Mitchell, contacted Thomas Kerr, a graduate of the Eastman School of Music and a piano instructor at Howard University. He agreed to play the orchestral reduction with me.

Kerr was a fine pianist, organist, and composer. We rehearsed the concerto in the Washington Conservatory of Music, which had two grand pianos, going through the work twice without stopping. The building that housed the conservatory on Ninth Street Northwest, in Washington, DC, was one that I had walked past many times as I went to Sunday school without being aware that it was operational.

The Baltimore Symphony was conducted by Reginald Stewart, a Canadian-born pianist. The concert was in a black high school auditorium in Baltimore. The orchestra had played the concerto with another soloist that season on its subscription series and was honed to the task. My performance went splendidly. The audience's response was enthusiastic. But Stewart, whose demeanor was cold and patronizing in the rehearsal, said nothing to me after the performance.

CONCERT PROMOTION

Since I didn't have a concert manager, I decided to be my own promoter. I had a black-and-white flyer printed with a photo and excerpts of reviews of my performances on it. When these were dispatched to black colleges, there were a few encouraging responses. Many of these colleges had lyceum programs. In some of these colleges were teachers whom I had known as students at Oberlin.

At Oakwood College in Alabama, a Seventh-Day Adventist institution, English professor Dr. Eva Dykes, who had taught at Howard University, recognized my name and arranged a concert for me. I had taken her course in English literature one summer for credit toward a master's degree. She had probably heard me play a recital on the concert series at Howard University.

For these recitals attendance was obligatory for all students. I was assured of a good house and a Steinway piano. At Alabama State College, the music department had purchased a new Steinway D Concert Grand. It was a superb instrument. I was the first pianist to use it for a recital. Audiences were always quiet and apparently attentive. As an artist, I became an ambassador of culture, something that was considered important in those days. My programs consisted of the same repertoire that I had played in concerts in New York, Washington, DC, Philadelphia, and other cities. At Oakwood College I enjoyed sitting at a long table in the midst of students and faculty. The dinner that was served on a Saturday evening included the most succulent yams that I have ever tasted. When I arrived the previous day, Dr. Dykes was most helpful in providing a meal for me during the fasting period of this religious institution that began on Friday at sunset.

MELLON ART GALLERY

Thomas Kerr was the first black pianist to play a recital at the Mellon Art Gallery in Washington, DC, which was dedicated in 1941. When I learned about this, I contacted Richard Bales, who had been appointed for life by the Mellon family as the director of music for the museum. Bales had studied at the Eastman School of Music. He was one of five conductors initially selected by Serge Koussevitzky for study at Tanglewood.

Bales told me about the obvious solicitations of Leonard Bernstein to curry favor with Koussevitzky that he found obsequious. He engaged me to play a recital in the East Garden Court of the Mellon Art Gallery a year after he had conducted my Adagio for String Orchestra (*Lyric for Strings*) in an uninspired, but successful performance. Bales was one of only a few genuinely sincere persons whom I had met at the beginning of my career.

The orchestra that he formed using members of the National Symphony was a chamber-sized ensemble of about twenty-five players. The setting for the Sunday concerts was a rectangular area with a concrete floor and massive pillars flanking one side of a courtyard. The audience, sitting on hard folding chairs, had a poor view of the performers since everyone was on the same level. Beautiful palm plants embellished the front of the space. The cathedral-like acoustics smudged everything in a cloud of uncontrollable resonance.

I played several piano recitals in the East Garden Court and one in the West Garden Court, which was identical in shape. Concerts that I gave in the Phillips Gallery and the Corcoran Art Gallery offered an intimate salon atmosphere that was more conducive for enjoyment by an audience. The acoustics were excellent for the performer.

DEAN DIXON

I wrote to Dean Dixon to express my interest in playing with his orchestra. He occasionally brought his ensemble, a makeshift group with some barely professional personnel, to other cities outside of New York for single concerts. He asked me to play the Beethoven Piano Concerto no. 4 with him in Baltimore. The only rehearsal was held in a cramped studio off of Broadway in Manhattan that had an upright piano. The concert was in the same auditorium in which I played the Second Brahms Concerto with the Baltimore Symphony. During the performance, there was an embarrassing moment at the end of the second movement of the Beethoven concerto. The cellos failed to come in on cue. Two years later I played the Tschaikowsky Piano Concerto no. 1 with Dixon and his orchestra at Hunter College. An old friend of Dean Dixon, Ingram Fox, remarked that the turgid accompaniment had handicapped my playing.

Dixon was about five feet, five and a half inches tall with an impressive head and a stout physique. He offered me the use of his piano when I was in New York. His mother invited me to stay for lunch after I had been practicing on his small M size Steinway grand. Breaking a string on it while playing the second movement of the Rachmaninoff Concerto no. 3 was embarassing. It was evident that Dixon had an enormous appetite after consuming more ground beef than I could eat in three meals.

He conducted without a baton, using broad, sweeping gestures that clearly defined the beat. His countenance was always unsmiling, stoically calm. His conversation was formal. (I was always called Mr. Walker.) He invariably wore a dark blue suit and a matching overcoat when he went out. He liked certain European conductors and pointedly remarked that Toscanini didn't understand how to conduct Brahms. I was both flattered and puzzled when he told me that I "had the best left hand that [he] had ever heard."

I became increasingly anxious about the dilemma in which I found myself. I had auditioned twice for Columbia Artists Management. I played Chopin and Prokovieff for several representatives in CAMI Hall. My performance of these works had been highly praised at my Town Hall debut recital. When Arthur Judson told me for a second time that he would like to hear me again after a few years, it was obvious that the Columbia Artists Management did not want to promote a black pianist. I had encountered a pressure-resistant stone wall. All that I had done to prepare myself for a concert career was of no avail.

WQXR, one of the classical FM stations in New York, broadcast live performances of pianists weekly in their studio at that time. Since I did not know how the performers were chosen for these programs, I called the radio station. An audition was arranged with Abram Chasins, who had been appointed director of WQXR. My knowledge of him was limited to a piano solo, "Rush Hour in Hong Kong," a quaint exercise in chinoiserie. He had taught piano at Curtis for nine years. His new bride, Constance Keene, was seated with him in the room at the audition. After playing the Chopin Barcarolle for them, his only intelligible comment was that he wouldn't want to schedule me before some of the other pianists who had been engaged to play. I was not offered a slot in his series of guest artists.

Traveling and Teaching

TRIP TO FONTAINEBLEAU

$\mathscr{I}$ decided to go to France to study with Robert Casadesus at the American School in Fontainebleau in the summer of 1947. I applied for a passport in Washington, DC. After I had returned home with the passport, I noticed that a clerk had changed the occupation that I had written on the application from "concert pianist" to "entertainer." I went back to the office the next day and demanded the reinstatement of "concert pianist."

The *Marine Tiger*, a boat crammed with students on all decks, provided the least expensive means of getting to France. World War II had ended. It was a ten-day voyage to cross the Atlantic, but at least we didn't have to fear the surreptitious U-boat. The devastation of the French countryside was evident during the train ride from Le Havre to Paris. Arriving at Fontainebleau, I found the town charming. The meals served at the American School reflected the economic stress of the postwar period. An egg on a plate of spinach almost caused me to regurgitate.

My first lesson with Casadesus was disappointing. He and Schnabel were among the few concert pianists who played Mozart concertos with major orchestras at that time. For my first lesson with him, I brought in the Mozart Sonata in A Major K. 331. He played along with me with his left hand. His assistant was even more exasperating. He assigned an étude in which the hands constantly crossed for four or five pages. The pianist, Grant Johannesen, who was also a student at the Ecole Americaine, was happily rummaging through French piano music that he didn't know.

Before I left the States, I had played a benefit concert in CAMI Hall in New York for Pakistan Relief. A woman who was in the audience contacted me when she learned that I would be going to France. She told me about a youth festival that would be held in the summer in Prague and said that if I were interested in going there, her organization would pay my expenses from Paris. I agreed to the proposal and decided to make the trip to Czechoslovakia after the end of the summer session in Fontainebleau. But since I was not happy with the instruction that I was receiving there, I obtained permission to leave the school at the beginning of the summer session and to receive a refund.

An interesting rendezvous occurred after the *Marine Tiger* docked in Le Havre when I first arrived in France. While waiting for my train to Paris, I saw a large, imposing man who was standing guard over a huge pile of luggage in the train station. We spoke. In introducing himself to me he said that he was Edric Connor, a bass-baritone who had come from London. He was born in Trinidad. Connor's voice had been likened to that of Paul Robeson. He told me that he was going to Prague. When I said that I would be going there later in the summer, he asked me to get in touch with him when I arrived.

PRAGUE

Leaving Fontainebleau and the American School, I reached Prague from Paris via the Orient Express. There were several American students who were also on the train. I located Edric after arriving in this beautiful city. It was teeming with happy-go-lucky students from many countries and young Czech survivors of the heinous German occupation of the country who were content to relish the green, unripened fruit sold from carts on the street. The taverns selling dark and light lager with limb-paralyzing aftereffects in the scorching temperature outside were filled with imbibing customers drowning their anxieties in the thick foam of their Pilsners.

Edric had met with the director of the radio station in Prague and had agreed to broadcast a program of songs. He asked me to accompany him. The program pleased the director. There was talk about organizing a tour of Czechoslovakia. The idea was appealing. A few days later we learned that there was a paper strike. Programs could not be printed.

The proposal collapsed, and I decided to return to Fontainebleau where I completed the summer session.

There was a piano competition in Prague during this youth festival. Among the Americans who were present for the events were Harriet Wingreen, who became the pianist for the New York Philharmonic, and Helen Kwalwasser, a violinist who joined the faculty of the music department of Temple University. The winner of the piano competition was a Russian pianist who was selected by a jury of Russians and Eastern Bloc representatives. (Contestants were required to play a work by a Czech composer.)

Several Americans who had come to Prague decided to present a short concert of American music to enlighten their hosts about music from the other side of the Iron Curtain. My contribution was to play the bass in a two-partnered version of Cole Porter's "Night and Day." The other pianist, Tella Marie Cole, had been my sister's roommate during her freshman year at Oberlin. The most unusual event was the appearance of some of the principal dancers of the Bolshoi Ballet— Raissa Struchkova, Olga Lepeshinskaya, and Maya Plisetskaya—whose fame transcended international borders.

RETURN TO FONTAINEBLEAU

A painter in the American School at Fontainebleau mentioned to me that he planned to go to the World's Fair in Brussels. This piqued my interest. We decided to take the train to Belgium over a weekend when there were no lessons or classes and to return the same day. The World's Fair had many exceptional displays. In a building that housed an art exhibit, there was a room containing some large canvases by the American painter Jackson Pollock. The duplication of techniques and color in these works was somewhat numbing. When I turned to look at a smaller painting of Pollock, I noticed two women ahead of me. One, slightly hunched in an unattractive earth-brown outfit and puppy-brown suede shoes, was Eleanor Roosevelt.

I had been dependent upon the painter who accompanied me to Brussels to keep track of the time. When we left the building, he consulted his train schedule. We had less than an hour to return to the train station to purchase tickets back to Paris. Huffing and puffing we ran into the depot knowing that if we missed the last train back to Paris, we would have to spend the night sleeping on a park bench. After buying my ticket, I sprinted to the platform, leaving my acquaintance behind. The train had just begun to move. I saw that the door to the mail car was open. I leaped into the cargo area to the astonishment of the men in that car. The painter returned to Fontainebleau the next afternoon.

During the final weeks of the summer session, Clifford Curzon, a former student of Mlle. Boulanger who was the director of the American School, arrived to give a master class for the piano students. I asked her if I could show Mr. Curzon my Piano Sonata no. 2. After the class ended, I played the sonata for him. Mlle. Boulanger apologetically told me later that Mr. Curzon was too busy to learn anything new.

PAUL ROBESON

The trip to Prague and an appearance at the site of a Paul Robeson concert in Peekskill, New York, that never materialized undoubtedly put me on Senator Joseph McCarthy's blacklist of un-American Americans. Having to flatten myself on the floor of a bus to avoid the vicious taunts and the stones thrown by the misguided citizenry and members of the American Legion lining the escape route from the vacant field where the concert had been scheduled was not something that I could have anticipated. I had been asked to perform with the folk singer Pete Seeger in 1949 on a program with Robeson. Reports about the unrest in Peekskill were sufficiently disturbing that Robeson's advisors warned him about the danger of driving to the town. The concert was rescheduled, but I was not present for it. The *New York Times* erroneously reported that I was there.

I never met Robeson, although I was invited to a reception that he attended. The adulation with which he was greeted by the attendees was sincere. He sang for the small gathering. His habit of singing with his right hand cupped behind his right ear was a little off-putting. Like Frank Sinatra, Robeson projected most of the songs in the same tempo. His last accompanist, Alan Booth, was a pianist who graduated from Oberlin College five years after I did. He was a good friend of my sister.

MOVE TO NEW YORK

The realization that living in Washington, DC, in 1947 would not help me to make contacts in New York prompted a discussion with my father about the options that I had. My father offered to buy a house for my sister and myself. She and I went house shopping on Long Island. Forest Hills in Queens was our first stop because it seemed to be one of the closest attractive locations to Manhattan. We entered a real estate office to find out what was affordable in that area, a predominantly Jewish community. An agent sitting at a desk, while scarcely looking up at us, stated that there was nothing available. He did not elaborate on his pronouncement. Housing discrimination was rampant in New York despite its illegality.

My father and I made a trip together to New York from Washington, DC. He and I found a small, well-proportioned home for sale by a real estate agency farther out on Long Island in St. Albans, New York. Several famous people have lived in that location—Jackie Robinson, Count Basie, Babe Ruth, Lena Horne, and W. E. B. Du Bois. My father bought the house for my sister and I so that we could continue to pursue a career in music. After an unfortunate experience at Curtis, my sister had begun to have piano lessons with Robert Goldsand in Manhattan. He proved to be a sympathetic and encouraging teacher.

NATIONAL CONCERT ARTISTS

In 1950, I had a conversation with Jacob Lateiner, a Vengerova student with whom I had been friends at Curtis. I expressed my disappointment at the rebuffs that I had received from Columbia Artists after having played two auditions for them. Several of my younger colleagues—Seymour Lipkin, Abba Bogin, and Jacob—had obtained management after I had made my "notable debut." Jacob spoke with Richard Leach of the National Concert Artists about me. When I contacted Leach, he offered me a contract. I did not have to play an audition.

Richard Leach was an artist representative whose primary area for promoting artists on the roster of the National Concert Artists was the Midwest. National Concert Artists and Columbia Artists were the largest concert managements in the country. He told me that he expected to have difficulty in selling a black classical pianist. His desire to help young artists was a personal commitment. If the other representatives with National Concert Artists had combined to make a serious effort to jump-start my career, I would have had considerably more engagements than I did.

Leach arranged for Abba Bogin and myself to meet William Kapell at Leach's apartment. It was directly across the street from the back of the Museum of Modern Art. This was a well-intentioned effort on his part to connect the younger generation of pianists. Leach had recently returned from Europe where he heard one of the last recitals of Dinu Lipatti. He had risked sipping unpasteurized milk in Switzerland. His enjoyment of it was short-lived. He became quite ill after he returned to the States.

After playing for Kapell, we listened to him doodle at the piano while talking about his fascination with the *Children's Corner Suite* of Debussy and the mazurkas of Chopin.

MORE NEW YORK RECITALS

I played two more recitals in Town Hall after my debut there. Both were sponsored by my father. On the first of these I played the Liszt Piano Sonata. The concert was well received. The second concert was in the fall of 1953. My mother, who had an operation to remove a kidney in 1941 and was unable to attend my graduation from Oberlin College, was in poor health. The foresight that my father had shown in purchasing a house for my sister and me made it possible for us to take care of her in New York.

It was my sole responsibility for two summers to provide everything for my mother, including cooking all of her meals. I took her by bus and subway into Manhattan for a daily injection by a wonderful physician, Dr. Emil Conason, the uncle of August (Augie) Meier, a classmate of my sister's and a scholar of black history. At the end of the summer I had less than two months to prepare for the third Town Hall recital in the fall after I brought my mother back to Washington, DC. The program for this concert consisted of the last Haydn Sonata in E-flat, Hob. 16/52; the Schumann Phantasie in C Major; the Prokovieff Toccata; and the Chopin Piano Sonata in B Minor.

The performance went extremely well. The precarious skips in the second movement of the Schumann Phantasie were negotiated perfectly. The Prokovieff Toccata created an explosive end to the first half of the program. Harold Schonberg, the piano guru for the *New York Times*, carefully avoided writing anything positive in the paper that could be quoted.

I met my father at his hotel the next day. He was returning to Washington, DC, by train. We took a cab to Penn Station. I was not aware that he had read the *New York Times* review. Standing on the platform with him as the engine approached, he said brusquely with a tinge of anger, "They will never give you what you deserve."

EUROPEAN TOUR

My father was aware that black classical singers had more opportunities in Europe than they had in the United States. It was a subject that he had brought up a few years earlier. With only a few concerts to prepare for in this country, I told my father that I would like to make a concert tour of Europe. Gerard Simon, an artist representative at National Concert Artists, booked halls for debut recitals with several additional concerts. In charging me a fee for each contract that he negotiated with the European managers, Simon violated the policy of the management. I was reminded of an unsolicited remark by Serkin who had said that "all managers are crooks." Debut recitals were arranged in Stockholm, Copenhagen, The Hague, Amsterdam, Frankfurt am Main, Milano, and London. There were additional concerts in Italy. I also recorded a program for radio stations in Lausanne and Basel, Switzerland.

In January 1954 I booked a passage on a new Dutch ocean liner making its maiden voyage to England. I had asked my father to let me wear his elegant dark brown Homburg hat for the trip. From London I took a train to Stockholm for the first concert of the tour. I was warmly received by the Swedish manager. Two days after my successful concert I had the opportunity of hearing Emil Gilels in a piano recital in the same hall. This performance occurred several years before he played in the United States. He strode out on the stage with his Star of Lenin insignia affixed to his lapel. His program consisted of Mozart, Beethoven, and Shostakovich. I also met Jorge Demus in Stockholm. He and Paul Badura-Skoda were among the first European pianists to play in the United States after World War II.

I had prepared two and a half recital programs. On one was the Chopin Piano Sonata in B Minor, op. 58; on the other was the Brahms Sonata in F Minor, op. 5. Two years earlier National Concert Artists had booked a recital for me at the Gardner Museum in Boston. After the recital a Boston dowager congratulated me on having the honor of playing there. When I submitted a program for a return visit the next year, I was asked to substitute another work for the Brahms sonata. I had just learned it and wanted to perform the sonata one time in public before going to Europe. The Gardner Museum informed me that programming the sonata would jeopardize any future engagements in that venue. I played the sonata.

From Stockholm I took the train to Copenhagen for my next recital. When I arrived in Copenhagen, my stomach had begun to give me problems. I tried to ease the cramping by drinking milk and eating fish. This did not help. I could barely straighten up when I walked out on the stage for the concert. The hall had been a museum at one time. The room backstage was lined with formidable suits of knights' armor and massive weaponry.

My success continued in Frankfurt am Main, where a newspaper flatly stated that my playing was both technically and musically superior to that of another pianist who had appeared recently in that auditorium. The hall was packed for my concert. I played the Brahms sonata on that recital. But the German manager claimed that he did not make any money from it.

My next recitals were in The Hague, Amsterdam, London, and Milano. A reviewer for my concert in The Hague found my playing completely different from what he described as the cold, American style of piano playing. In Milano, half of the audience came backstage at intermission to greet me with great approbation. The manager of my concerts in Italy was very excited about the reception that I received. She told me that Friedrich Gulda was upset because he did not have any success there. Another concert that I heard him play demonstrated his ability to play all of the notes cleanly more than anything else.

The London concert was well attended. But the review, unlike those that I had received in Europe, consisted of only a few lines. After a concert in Bologna, I was invited to play the Beethoven Piano Concerto no. 4 with an orchestra there. The constant cramping in my stomach forced me to decline the offer. When I returned to Washington,

DC, my father quickly diagnosed the symptoms. I had an ulcer. I was unable to accept an engagement to play the Rachmaninoff Concerto no. 3 in Birmingham, England, during the next season.

RETURN TO THE UNITED STATES

Realizing that the lack of concert opportunities combined with my physical condition had created a serious problem for me, my father suggested that I accept a teaching position in a college. The minister of our church in Washington, DC, Reverend Earl Harrison, knew Albert Dent, the president of Dillard University in New Orleans, and told my father about a vacancy in the music department there. I applied for the job and was accepted for the position of instructor in piano and theory.

After I returned from Europe, I had begun to work on a piano sonata. For my Town Hall debut in 1945, I had composed a set of three pieces. The first one, "Prelude," is published with "Danse Exotique," the short work that I had composed when I was eighteen. The title of it was changed to "Caprice." "Touchpiece," a theme with variations, was written for my second Town Hall concert to conclude the program. After writing these short works, I felt compelled to compose a large-scale work. I decided to find material that would define the work as an American sonata. It occurred to me that the use of quartal harmony would also add some distinction to it.

PIANO SONATA NO. 1

The principal theme of the first movement of my First Piano Sonata incorporates intervals of fourths, thirds, and seconds. Contrary to the inaccurate statements made in several doctoral dissertations about the intervallic content, there is no consistency in the use of the interval of a fourth. (Where were the doctoral advisors for these students?) The sonata manages to integrate all of these intervals without having a predominance of one interval. The second movement is a theme and variations based on a folk song, "O Bury Me beneath the Willow," that

I found in Carl Sandburg's *Songbag*. The harmonization of the theme uses fourths and other intervals.

The same boat, the *Marine Tiger*, that took me to Le Havre in the summer of 1947, also brought me back six weeks later to the United States. Two days before we were scheduled to dock in the harbor in New York, the purser of the *Marine Tiger* asked me if I would arrange an informal concert for the students aboard the ship. When I began to consider whom I might ask to participate in this program, I remembered conversations that I had with a brilliant black student. We met on the boat going to France. I spotted him in the mass of students on the return trip. He had taught anatomy in a California state university and had told me that he enjoyed singing in barber shop quartets. I spoke to him about the program that I had been asked to present. He offered to find three other persons who could make up a quartet. I approached two piano students who were at Fontainebleau when I was there and asked them if they would be willing to play on this hastily arranged program. They agreed to do so. I concluded the event by playing two Chopin études on the upright piano. Bobbing with each dip of a wave, it had its moments of instability in the rough waters of the Atlantic Ocean.

The barber shop quartet formed by the anatomy teacher was initially derided by a black medical student with whom I had also become acquainted. But the performance by the quartet on the boat was a very effective part of the short program.

It came as a revelation to me, as I read through all of the folk songs in Carl Sandburg's collection when I was at home again in St. Albans, to discover that the melody of one of the songs sung by the barber shop quartet had been documented. The title of the song is "Lisa." I appropriated this song for the first contrasting theme in the arch form of the third movement of my piano sonata. I completed the work the day before my departure for New Orleans. That had been the deadline that I had arbitrarily set.

TEACHING IN NEW ORLEANS

In September of 1953, when I went south to Dillard University to teach piano and theory, I had already severed my ties with the National Concert

Artists. A few months before I left for New Orleans, I was surprised to be contacted by the Harold Shaw Concert Management without having met anyone there. I was given a contract to play several concerts in southern colleges. Shaw, the founder of this management had worked as an artist representative for Columbia Artists. He had snared Horowtiz from Columbia Artists and booked him for several years.

Two days before I was supposed to play my first concert under the management of Shaw Concerts, I had a severe ulcer attack. This occurred after I had been at Dillard University for only two weeks. I sent a telegram to the concert bureau in New York and explained my inability to fulfill the engagements that they had obtained for me. I never received a reply from this management. I was not optimistic about the possibility of playing concerts again.

I made an appointment with a white physician in New Orleans and was told to use the rear entrance to his office. Determined not to be subjected to the humiliation of this debasing southern code, I rang the front doorbell and entered his office from the street. I spent a month in a hospital receiving the primitive treatment given in those days for my condition. When I left the hospital, I was still too weak to do anything. Without a refrigerator in my room it was virtually impossible to keep the diet of milk and cream, which was placed on the windowsill in the evening, from turning sour in the hot, humid atmosphere of New Orleans. The corrugated metal buildings on the campus contributed to raising the temperature inside the rooms considerably.

The chairman of the music department at Dillard University, Mel Bryant, was very solicitous in his concern for my well-being. He took over my classes. When I returned to teaching, I enjoyed the experience of working with students who had limited skills and colleagues who worked strenuously to offset the deficiencies of an economically strapped institution. Bryant had to plead directly to the president of the university for items as inexpensive as chalk for classrooms. Black colleges were almost totally dependent on the charitable dispositions of white politicians.

In the spring of 1954 I heard about a shoe sale in one of the stores in downtown New Orleans from some of the professors at Dillard University. It was an accepted fact that white-owned stores would not allow a black person to try on a hat. But this particular store was allowing black customers to buy shoes. I made my first and only trip from the campus of the Dillard University to the downtown section of

New Orleans. (I never saw the famous French Quarter when I was in that city.) I purchased a pair of brown shoes, although I was not overly fond of the color. (I thought that a dark polish would make them more acceptable.) I took a seat in the front of the bus headed back to Dillard. As the bus filled up with white passengers who were clustered around me, I would have been expected to move to the back of the bus. In my weakened condition, I decided to keep my seat in defiance of the expected. This was nine months before the Rosa Parks incident in Birmingham, Alabama. I am sure that other black persons have protested similarly without attracting the attention that sparked the civil revolt in that state.

The resolve that I mustered in New Orleans had surfaced on a trip a few years earlier when I was going to play in West Virginia. A person traveling by rail from Philadelphia to a southern state had to change trains in Washington, DC, or move to the Jim Crow car that seated only black persons. Since I did not have to change trains, I remained in my seat. The conductor took my ticket and asked me to move. Looking out of the window, I ignored him. Nothing more was said.

Before the end of the second semester at Dillard University, I read an article in the *New York Times* that outlined a new doctoral program devised by Dr. Howard Hanson, director of the Eastman School of Music. The doctor of musical arts (DMA) degree was created for instrumentalists and composers who did not want to pursue a doctoral degree in musicology. In a flash I knew that this program would supplement my performance background by giving me superior academic credentials. All of the teachers at Dillard University had master's degrees. I had not completed my degree. This was reflected in my salary of three thousand dollars for the year. I applied for admission into the program. When I was admitted, I requested a fellowship to cover my tuition. This was also granted. I had expected to go to Eastman in the fall of 1954.

RETURN TO WASHINGTON, DC

Two days before my departure from New Orleans, I received a telegram from my father. In it he said that he would be in the hospital when I arrived. The key to the house would be under the straw mat in the vestibule.

The house was empty when I arrived by train in Washington, DC. My mother was being cared for by my sister in New York. Finding the key and opening the door, I dropped my bag in the hall and immediately took a taxi to the hospital. I met Dr. Gusack, my father's doctor, a compassionate practitioner, in the hall as he left my father's room. He told me that my father had cancer. He had only a month to live.

For three months I took care of my father with the occasional assistance of one of his patients, who was a nurse, and my uncle, who was handicapped by an arm injury. On the morning of the last day of his life, he made a prophetic statement. He said, "This is the day." While feeding him prunes that he had requested for breakfast, he lapsed into a coma that I knew would lead to his expiration. It has been a source of comfort to me in knowing that I gave both of my parents their last meal before they departed from this world.

Two weeks before my father's death, he had given me specific instructions for his funeral. When I went to McGuire's Funeral Home to secure their services, the owner, without any hesitation, asked me to select a casket and to tell him how many funeral cars would be necessary for my family and friends. He would take it care of it (gratis). Before this encounter I obviously had only a limited awareness of the powerful impact that my father had on the black community in Washington, DC.

DOCTORAL PROGRAM AT EASTMAN

The death of my father forced me to delay my entrance into the doctoral program at Eastman. But I was granted permission to begin in January of 1955. I remained in Washington, DC, for three months to manage my father's affairs. During that time I did not touch a piano.

I drove to Rochester in a black DeSoto four-door sedan, a lower tier Chrysler product that I purchased a few days before leaving St. Albans, New York, for Eastman. The green car that I had placed a deposit on was sold by a dishonest salesman to another customer before I came up with the balance for it. I had weighed a couple of options for getting to Rochester. It became clear to me that I could not make the seven-hour trip by train with the clothes and musical materials that I would need.

When I arrived in Rochester in January of 1955, the dean of students at Eastman, Flora Burton, told me that finding an apartment in that city would be futile. She intimated that housing discrimination was a serious problem there. The YMCA that was directly across from the Eastman Theatre was a very convenient alternative. There was a cafeteria on the second floor that served breakfast and dinner.

The door to the annex at Eastman where practice rooms were located on the second floor was opened exactly at 8:00 a.m. Sibley Library occupied the first floor. The short walk from the YMCA after breakfast at 7:15 a.m. enabled me to be one of the first persons to enter the annex every morning. The practice rooms were small. My first glimpse of the upright pianos in each room caused me to question my decision to come to Eastman. But when I entered a room, I discovered that the piano was new and the action was stiff—this was my preference in a piano. I never looked for another room.

The competition for practice pianos wasn't as keen as it had been at Oberlin. I could leave what became "my room" for a half hour at a time and return to find it unoccupied. The undergrads may have been a bit intimidated in knowing that I had been a Serkin student with a concert career behind me.

By consuming lunch quickly in the cafeteria at Eastman, there was always enough time before classes resumed to play two games of table tennis on an ancient table with John Boda, a doctoral candidate in composition with a wicked forehand smash from his pen-hold grip.

I became acquainted with three interesting and very amicable persons who frequented the cafeteria in the YMCA. Bob worked at Eastman Kodak and studied piano at Eastman with Jose Echaniz. Bill, who taught piano in the Preparatory Department at Eastman, was a doctoral candidate and a young bearded professor who taught English at the River Campus of the University of Rochester. We would meet at a table every evening during the week for dinner. This was always a delightful occurrence at the end of the day.

My room on the third floor of the YMCA was only large enough to accommodate a bed and desk. The son of a colleague of my father, Dr. Bertram Phillips, had prescribed for me before I left Washington, DC, his own potion containing various soothing ingredients. He recommended this medication to his patients with stomach problems in Jamaica, British West Indies, where he lived.

I had continued to drink a combination of milk and cream for my ulcer after I left New Orleans. This diet increased my weight by over twenty pounds. But it also left me extremely weak. After my classes at Eastman, I would collapse, exhausted, on the bed before I could recover sufficiently to study. I discontinued the diet when I decided to avoid eating meat for two years. This carnivorous temptation was considerably reduced by my fear of becoming incapacitated again.

Eastman Faculty

I chose Jose Echaniz for my piano teacher. Mr. Echaniz was a warm and gregarious person, a concert pianist who had been a child prodigy in Cuba. He had also been the conductor of the Grand Rapids Symphony in Michigan. Echaniz had a delightfully deprecatory sense of humor. I was treated as a colleague by him rather than as a graduate student. Upon hearing me play, he arranged an audition with the piano faculty that would allow me to obtain an artist diploma in addition to a doctoral degree. When he had a recording session of piano music by South American composers in New York, he invited me to attend it. He came to visit my sister and her husband at our home in St. Albans. We talked well into the night after they had retired for the evening.

The fellowship that I received from Eastman was for a job as a coach in the opera department. Leonard Treash was the director. I would attend every opera class and I was available for any additional assistance as an accompanist when it was requested by the singers. Singers in the class prepared roles in the standard repertoire and in contemporary operas composed by composition teachers on the faculty. Howard Hanson's opera, *Merry Mount*, was revived for a performance in the newly renovated Eastman Theatre. The huge chandelier inside the hall had been precariously dangling several stories above the parquet. It had to be stabilized. This was a part of the restoration of the hall. The students whom I coached in the opera class performed in *Merry Mount*. Howard Hanson conducted the orchestra.

I had planned to complete the DMA degree as quickly as possible by taking summer courses after the regular academic year. A week after the first summer session had begun, a telegram from my sister informed me that my mother was seriously ill. I left Rochester the next day and did not return until the fall semester. My mother, who was in a coma, made a remarkable recovery. A miracle had occurred. We learned from a very empathetic nurse in the small, private hospital where she had been taken,

Mr. Echaniz's piano class, Eastman School of Music, 1955–1956

that her eyes had opened. When my sister and I arrived at the hospital to see her, she looked up at us without turning her head, her gaze childlike and serene, as if to tell us that she had been in a very quiet place.

My mother was confined to a wheelchair for the remainder of her life. The therapy provided to stroke victims was not made available to her. It was very unfortunate that her doctor and my sister did not explore methods for her rehabilitation that would lead to a full or partial recovery of her ability to function normally. The treatment that she received from Dr. Conason when she was under my care for two summers was very effective. She could walk then. But she was allowed to lapse into old, debilitating habits when I brought her back to Washington, DC. My father never reconciled himself to the change in her mental and physical condition. He tried hard but unsuccessfully to adjust to the imbalance that my mother's illness had created in the maintenance of the household.

I was able to complete all of the doctoral requirements in December of 1956. These included three full-length piano recitals and a lecture recital with all of the prescribed courses. For the artist diploma, I played the Piano Concerto no. 2 of Brahms with Hanson conducting the Eastman Philharmonia Orchestra. The reviewer for the *Rochester Times* called the performance one of the finest that he had ever heard.

Dr. Eugene Selhorst was appointed to the graduate faculty. He taught a doctoral seminar and a course in sixteenth-century counterpoint. For the final exam of the counterpoint class we were required to complete several exercises in three-part writing and to write an exposition for a four-voice fugue. Three hours were allocated for the completion of the test. I finished the exam in forty-five minutes. As I left the room, I saw Donald White, another theory instructor. He asked me why I was not taking the graduate exam. I told him that I had finished it.

I received an A for the exam and the course. Several months earlier, in a casual conversation, Selhorst had surprised me by stating that he wanted me to achieve an academic level that was comparable to my pianistic ability. He should have known that I had an A average from the courses that I had taken.

In the summer of 1957 I was invited to give a series of piano recitals in Trinidad. The sponsor for these concerts was the director of the public library in Port-au-Prince. He was determined to bring cultural events to this island. After I played two recitals in the library, the third

Three Applaude

By HARVEY SOUTHGATE

A MASTERLY performance of the Brahms second concerto for piano and orchestra, with George Walker at the piano, in Kilbourn Hall last night brought the fifth and final Eastman School concerto program of the season to an appropriately exciting close. Walker, a candidate for the degree doctor of musical arts and the Artist's Diploma, collaborated with the Eastman-Rochester Orchestra, conducted by Dr. Howard Hanson, in a performance that surely will be remembered among the mostly warmly applauded in the long series of these concerto programs presented by advanced Eastman School students. Last night's was the 110th in the series. As usual a capacity audience was on hand.

This was indeed a performance of genuine professional caliber of one of the most nobly proportioned compositions of its kind. Here is the mature Brahms creating a work of art from a grand design that takes form before the ears of the listener in somewhat the way that a building rises before the eyes. Here is symmetry, power and perfectly meshed piano and orchestral patterns.

Mr. Walker set forth the piano core of the work with the right intellectual approach, coupled with a dazzling technical performance that realized the larger emotional context. There are moments when the composer himself is more concerned with mechanics than with beauty, but all in all this is a vastly exciting work and was so played last night by both soloist and orchestra.

Review of Brahms Piano Concerto no. 2, March 2, 1956

concert was cancelled. There wasn't sufficient interest in the efforts that he made to acquaint the local populace with standard piano repertoire. One of my predecessors on his series was Jascha Heifetz.

Dissertation

In the fall semester of 1956, Howard Hanson conveyed to one of the theory instructors that he wanted a class created to study the ideas that he was expounding in a new book. For those of us who thought that we had almost completed the requirements for the DMA degree, another course seemed to be an unwanted imposition. The basic material of the book focused on identifying the intervallic content of chord structures. The instructor, Robert Sutton, managed to keep one chapter ahead of the class as he received the latest pages from Hanson.

Hanson had another idea that I found more attractive. Instead of making a dissertation a requirement for a DMA degree, he proposed alternative projects that could be substituted for this stipulation. The student, if he wished, could compose a work or make an arrangement of one.

I decided to write another piano sonata. My intention was to demonstrate that the sonata could be harmonically consistent in its use of thirds. The Piano Sonata no. 2 begins with a theme that is the mirror image in diminution of a ground bass from which six variations are constructed. The second movement corresponds to a scherzo in ABA form. The writing is mostly in three parts. The third movement is monothematic. It is characterized by an expanding figuration in parallel octaves above powerful chords. At the end of the fourth movement that is in sonatina form, there is a recurrence of the initial motive of the first movement. This creates a cyclic effect.

In composing the sonata, all of the ideas that I had considered materialized. After completing it, I made a version for two pianos. This was the dissertation that I defended in my final orals before Hanson and several members of the music faculty. The Second Piano Sonata is dedicated to my father.

Trombone Concerto

A conversation with Porter Poindexter, a black trombone student of Emory Remington, provided me with the incentive to compose a trombone concerto that I would be able to hear immediately after its completion. He explained to me that he didn't want to play the Rimsky-Korsakov concerto that was originally written for trombone and band. He had been selected as an outstanding performer in his class to appear as a soloist with the student orchestra, the Eastman Philharmonia. I offered to compose a concerto for him if he would play it, although I had never heard a concerto for this instrument. The composition of my trombone concerto went rapidly. Not a single note has ever been changed since it was finished.

I was very concerned about having the parts extracted in time for the first rehearsal of the work. The copyist, whom I chose, another trombonist, was a friend of Poindexter. He had taken a calligraphy course at Eastman. In order to make the deadline, a second student was recruited as a copyist. The calligraphy of the third movement is distinctly cruder than that of the first two movements. But the cost of the copying, which I paid for, was well worth the result—a world premiere.

Hanson began to conduct the first rehearsal of the concerto without a baton. For the next two rehearsals and the concert he used a short stick. He was apparently more comfortable in using a baton for the numerous meter changes, although it was rumored that he had a back problem. The performance of the trombone part in the student concert in Kilbourn Hall was marred by many flubbed notes. Porter, who always seemed to be self-possessed, was clearly nervous and unsure of himself. But the response by the audience to the work was electric. The hall exploded with applause after the performance. I received three curtain calls.

The Trombone Concerto has been called the finest work for this medium. Emory Remington, Poindexter's teacher, stated that he knew only one trombonist other than Poindexter who could play my concerto. (He was referring to John Marcellus, who was then the first trombone player in the National Symphony. Marcellus played the concerto about twenty years later with the U.S. Navy Band. It was embarrassingly bad.) That observation would not be applicable today. Trombonists have become more technically proficient. But the concerto is still a demanding work that does not resort to gimmicks.

It was reported that Poindexter was invited to audition for the recording that Columbia Records planned to make of the Trombone Concerto. He declined. Denis Wick, the principal trombonist of the London Symphony, had heard the Eastman performance from a wire recording obtained by another Eastman trombonist, Ray Premru. Ray had become the bass trombonist of the London Symphony when he moved to England. Wick was contracted by Columbia Records to play the solo part with the London Symphony. His recording on an LP with the London Symphony has been superseded by a CD on BIS records by Christian Lindberg. James DePreist, who conducted the concerto with Lindberg as the soloist in Sweden, deemed the Trombone Concerto a "masterpiece." Eastman allowed me to continue as a coach in the opera department after I had completed the doctoral degree in December of 1956.

Cello Sonata

An unusual inquiry was made when I was in my practice room in the Eastman Annex. A young woman knocked on the door and introduced herself to me. She was looking for a composer who would be willing to write something for her. She said that she was a cellist. All of the composers whom she had tried to contact were busy. Someone suggested my name. She said that she could only pay twenty-five dollars to commission a work from me. I said that this was acceptable, and I began to work on the first movement of a cello sonata.

When I had finished the movement several weeks later, I attempted to locate her. I was told that she had left Rochester with her husband. I continued to work on the cello sonata, adding a slow movement and a fugue for the third movement. I have never seen or heard from this person since that brief encounter. The account of this meeting was mentioned in a review of a recital by Janos Starker that appeared in the *New York Daily News*. Starker had programmed the Cello Sonata on a concert that he gave in the Metropolitan Museum of Art in New York.

FULBRIGHT FELLOWSHIP

With no desire to find another teaching position, I applied for a Fulbright Fellowship to study piano in Paris. As a backup in case I didn't receive the Fulbright, I also submitted an application to the John Hay Whitney Foundation for a fellowship to study composition in Paris. The latter had never been granted to a composer before I received it. My Cello Sonata was the work that I submitted. When I received both fellowships, I requested that the funding for the John Hay Whitney be delayed for a year.

After I arrived in Paris, the Fulbright Commission held a meeting for all of the students who had fellowships in music. The director told us that we could select a private instructor if we did not want to enroll in the Conservatoire or the Ecole Normale de Musique. Having this freedom of choice meant that I would not be required to study with another disappointing French pianist. I informed the Fulbright Commission that I wanted to study with Mlle. Nadia Boulanger. This meant a commitment to concentrate on composition for the entire year. The success achieved by the works that I had composed at Eastman spurred me to make this decision.

I lived in the American House of Cité Universitaire for two years. On the third floor of the building were a few rather large rooms for artists and musicians. I was fortunate in obtaining a studio with an Erard grand piano in my second year in the American House. The isolation of the studio from the bustling activities and noise on the floors below provided an ideal atmosphere for composing and for practicing the piano. The noise from the traffic snarls on the busy boulevard was considerably less on the third floor. Yuen Yuey Chinn, a painter born in China, had an adjacent studio. I purchased one of his paintings, sight unseen, when I began to teach at Rutgers University. We are still friends.

MLLE. NADIA BOULANGER

At my first lesson with Mlle. Boulanger I showed her three songs. Quickly perusing the first one, "A Bereaved Maid," she said, "This is a masterpiece. You are a composer. Don't you mean F# here?" (There was an accidental missing in the vocal part.) This song is a setting of an anonymous fifteenth-century text. She was equally impressed with the two piano sonatas that I showed her next. Her preference was the first one. I doubt that she understood the second sonata, which has become a favorite of many pianists. She thought that the syncopation in the last movement was a little excessive. She advised me to use less of it "although you can do it better than most [composers]."

The Piano Sonata no. 2 is somewhat less demanding than my first piano sonata, which is formidable for even the best pianists. She asked me to play the Piano Sonata no. 1 on one of her musicals in Paris and suggested that I make a choral version of "The Bereaved Maid." This arrangement is incorporated in my *Three Lyrics for Chorus*.

After the performance of my Piano Sonata no. 1, Mlle. Boulanger asked me to make a copy of the sonata. She personally mailed it to the Lili Boulanger Competition chaired by Walter Piston, another former pupil, at Harvard University. Although the work did not receive the prize, she asked me to play it again the next summer after arranging a scholarship for me to attend the American School in Fontainebleau in 1958. The works that I completed in the one and a half years that I spent in Paris included a second violin and piano sonata and my *Address for Orchestra*.

The Second Violin Sonata is totally different from the graduation work that I composed at Curtis. It is a sonata in one continuous movement with a fugal exposition presented after the opening section. The second section contains rapid passages for both instruments in sixteenth notes. The third section is a recitativo. The introduction recurs, greatly intensified, in the final section of the work. One of the chief difficulties in this sonata is the coordination of the piano and violin parts. The spare writing in the fugue requires a precise observance of each eighth note. Otherwise, the synchronization of the two parts will be irretrievably lost.

I was determined to avoid being influenced by French music when I was in Paris, although I have always been fond of certain works of Debussy, Ravel, and Franck. Works of these composers were frequently played on Radio France, along with Beethoven, and they were often heard on orchestral concerts. But they represented music of the past, music using a distinguishable harmonic language that I would not employ. I had observed before coming to Europe that composers who wrote songs using French texts invariably created music that sounded French.

When the sonata was published by Associated Music, I sent a copy of it to Efrem Zimbalist. A brief note from Mrs. Zimbalist (he had married) expressed her husband's inability to understand the work. But they hoped that I would be more communicative in future compositions.

The four-note motive that permeates the first movement of the *Address for Orchestra* is the core element in a proclamatory statement. Its use in a fugal statement transforms it into playful iterations. In the contrasting lyrical theme, the rhythm of the four notes becomes accompanimental. The brooding second movement is followed by a passacaglia of grand proportions that is based on a modulating ground bass containing eleven different notes. Sixteen variations exploit all of the sections of the orchestra. A pedal point established by the timpani contributes to the robustness of the climax.

Trip to Fontainebleau, Summer 1958

Unlike many of Mlle. Boulanger's students—Copland, Piston, Thomson, Carter, Harris, and others—I was never subjected to counterpoint or harmony lessons. Boulanger obviously sensed that the skill exhibited in the works that I showed her indicated a very strong technical background. (It wasn't necessary for me to tell her that I had over nine years of music theory.)

Few, if any, of her students would have had a comparable indoctrination. Some of my most frequently performed works, the *Lyric for Strings*, the Piano Sonatas nos. 1 and 2, my Trombone Concerto, and the Cello Sonata were composed without any tutorial assistance before I began to study with Boulanger. She never corrected anything or suggested the rewriting of any passage during any of my visits to 36 rue Ballu.

At Fontainebleau, Boulanger's theory students made late submissions of exercises by shoving them under her door at 7:00 a.m. I was free to bring to my lessons anything that I chose. In the course of looking at my *Address for Orchestra* she said, "Your music has power."

Hanson and Scalero

Nadia Boulanger was the first person to acknowledge and praise my gift for musical composition. Hanson had said nothing to me after the enthusiastic reception that my Trombone Concerto received. I never had a composition lesson with him or any composition teacher at Eastman. I did, however, play my Piano Sonata no. 1 for a composition class for graduate students that he taught. This was done to acquaint him with my previous experience in composing for the piano after I had proposed another piano sonata for my dissertation. I did not have a doctoral advisor.

When I played the sonata for Hanson, he pointed out what he described as the inconsistent use of quartal harmony. Although he was an astute administrator, he didn't realize that consistency can be the bane of mediocrity. Pentatonic and whole-tone scales have an exotic appeal. But the prolonged use of them induces blandness and limits the composer's capacity for achieving dramatic effects. Consistent quartal usage replicates the same effect. Hanson's criticism was at odds with the highly positive response of his class to the piano sonata.

It is difficult to ascertain what Scalero could hear beyond triads and seventh chords. He was certainly a very closed-minded individual.

One of his students, Paul Garabedian, unhesitatingly called him a fascist. The only compliment that I received from Scalero (if it could be called such) was that after having studied with him, I would be able to write better arrangements of spirituals than those that were sung.

Boulangerie

Before I decided to discontinue my lessons with Mlle. Boulanger, I had begun to feel that preparing something to show her had become burdensome. Her remarks were limited to saying, "Keep going." (Shades of Berio's Sinfonia.) Leaving Mlle. Boulanger was not the end of our relationship. She continued to correspond with me after I returned to the United States.

It would be impossible to dispute the contribution that Mlle. Boulanger has made toward the musical education of many American and European students. Her technical expertise in solfege, theory, and counterpoint was remarkable. Equally inspiring was her passion for musical expression that had no counterpart in the academic circles of this country. Many of her students never progressed beyond the exercises that she prescribed. Her teaching of composition was not marked by dogma. But I never heard her mention or discuss the important element of form that is essential to establishing not only the shape of a composition, but its length. The "Boulangerie" was not a group of conformists. To suggest that she imposed a style of composition, as many have implied in writing about her, conveys a totally inaccurate account of her influence.

Two of my closest friends in Paris were a young Canadian couple, Boyd Mcdonald, a pianist, and his wife, Sylvia, a soprano. They always attended the Wednesday class held in Mlle. Boulanger's apartment. Folding chairs were set up in the room where she taught composition. About fifteen to twenty students sat elbow to elbow in front of her organ to listen for an hour to a rambling lecture, ostensibly without any plan or focus. We were asked to purchase several compositions for the class. But they were never analyzed and some were never mentioned again. The tone of the lecture was inspirational with frequent references to one of her favorite writers, Paul Valery. Occasionally, Mlle. Boulanger would pose a question to the students. Everyone would freeze in anticipation of being asked to respond. But the question invariably became a rhetorical one.

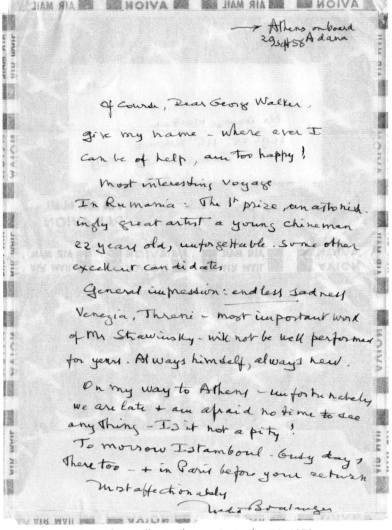

→ Athens on board
29sd58 Adana

Of course, Dear Georg Walker,

give my name – where ever I
can be of help, am too happy !

Most interesting voyage
In Rumania : The 1st prize, an astonishingly great artist a young chineman
22 years old, unforgettable . Some other
excellent candidates

General impression : endless sadness
Venezia, Threni – most important work
of Mr Strawinsky – will not be well performed
for years . Always himself, always new .

On my way to Athens – unfortunately
we are late + am afraid no time to see
anything – Is it not a pity !
Tomorrow Istamboul . busy days,
There too – + in Paris before your return
Most affectionately
Nadia Boulanger

Letter from Mlle. Boulanger, September 29, 1958

Another friend and Boulanger student, James Yannatos, became
the conductor of a chamber orchestra that presented a few concerts in
the American House at the Cité Universitaire in Paris. I asked Jimmy if
he would program my *Lyric for Strings* on one of his concerts. He suggested that I conduct it. After one rehearsal of the score, I conducted

the work from memory. After the concert Mme. Gaby Casadesus, who was in the audience, warmly praised the music and suggested that I compose a piano concerto for her. Jimmy, after his return to the United States, became the long-term conductor of the Harvard-Radcliff Orchestra.

Mlle. Boulanger invited her Wednesday class to attend a rehearsal of one of the French orchestras that Leonard Bernstein had been engaged to conduct. The rehearsal was scheduled to begin at 10:00 a.m. At 10:25 Bernstein still had not shown up.

The first work to be played was Bach's Brandenburg Concerto no. 5. When he finally arrived, Bernstein began to conduct and play the solo keyboard part from memory. In the middle of the first movement he couldn't remember the solo part. He didn't have a score. (Up the creek without a paddle.) The orchestra decided to proceed with the next work, Gershwin's "American in Paris." It was reported later that Bernstein had been shopping for a red leather jacket prior to the rehearsal.

Mlle. Boulanger also invited the class to hear a preconcert performance of Elliott Carter's String Quartet no. 1, a long work, repetitious in its soloistic gestures, played by a French string quartet. (I heard the premiere of his Second String Quartet performed by the Juilliard String Quartet after I had returned to New York.)

Boulez had established his Domaine Musical concerts in Paris when I was there. His lack of professional conducting skill was apparent in movements that involved the twitching of his shoulders as much as the flexing of his hands. The batonless technique that he has refined may have been improved with instruction from a teacher who suggested more conventional gestures that were less spastic. When Boulez left his position as the music director of the New York Philharmonic, some orchestra members were critical of his conducting. At a concert on which Stravinsky's Pulcinella was played, the ensemble disintegrated. The orchestra bailed him out of the disorder.

Mlle. Boulanger was always extremely discreet in her informal afternoon salons (not the Wednesday class). She would not be drawn into sizing up Boulez. She understood the consequences of political infighting. Everyone knew that her allegiance to Stravinsky was inviolable. She showed no interest in dodecaphonic music. I doubt that the fermata-laden score of "Le Marteau sans Maitre" of Boulez that I heard in Paris before it was introduced to American audiences had any appeal for her.

Spoleto

The first Spoleto Festival created by Gian-Carlo Menotti began in the summer of 1958. I received one of the two grants offered by the United States Information Service to attend the festival. Upon my arrival, I sought out my former orchestration teacher, Gian-Carlo Menotti. He asked me to accompany a violinist, Michael Tree (formerly Appelbaum), who needed an accompanist for his recital. Mrs. Zimbalist at Curtis had arranged his trip to Spoleto, and that of his wife, Marlena Kleinman, as a wedding present. When I met Michael, he seemed more absorbed with a motorbike.

Since I didn't have a tuxedo for the concert, Thomas Schippers, the conductor in residence for a performance of Verdi's *Macbeth*, fitted me with his full dress suit. I saw Samuel Barber for the last time at this concert. Several years later Tree appeared to have abandoned the violin by becoming the violist in the Guarneri String Quartet. This ensemble consists of four Curtis graduates.

PARIS 1958–1959

My second year in Paris was made possible by the John Hay Whitney Foundation. Mlle. Boulanger had recommended me to the Fulbright Commission for an extension of my fellowship for an additional year. But the extension was given to a piano student, John Price, who spent most of his time consorting with friends or playing cards with the director of the Fulbright Commission. When I discontinued my lessons with Boulanger in the spring of 1959, I decided to play recitals in The Hague, Amsterdam, and Italy again before returning to the United States.

NEW YORK 1960–1961

In March of 1960 I gave the premiere of my Piano Sonata no. 2 in a Town Hall recital. Harold Schonberg of the *New York Times* was very favorably impressed by the work that has been called a "masterpiece" by many artists and musicians. In the fall of 1960 the Dalcroze School of Music offered me a job teaching piano in their school. The meager

GEORGE
WALKER

PIANIST

Since his first appearance in New York which the New York Times described as "a notable debut recital", George Walker's success has been equally divided between performance and composition. His numerous awards include Fulbright and John Hay Whitney Fellowships in composition and his works have been performed throughout the United States, Europe and in South America. He holds a doctorate degree in music from the University of Rochester.

"As an interpreter of music, he will rank with the outstanding musicians of our time."

—*Het Vrije Volk, Amsterdam*

"He has all the valid requisites for becoming famous."

—*L'Italia, Milan*

"A technical competence and sensitivity rarely heard."

N. Y. Times

Town Hall, Thursday evening, March 3, 1960 at 8:30 P.M.

PROGRAM

Sonata in C minor, K. 457 .... Mozart
Sonata in F minor (Appassionata), Opus 57 .... Beethoven

INTERMISSION

Sonata no. 2 .... George Walker
(First New York Performance)
Two Etudes, Opus 10 .... Chopin
Funérailles .... Liszt
Gaspard de la Nuit .... Ravel

Steinway Piano

Ticket Prices: Orchestra $2.50, $1.75; Balcony $1.75, $1.15
Loges $3.00 per seat. Tax included.

Now on sale at Steinway Box Office, 111 West 57th Street, New York 19, N. Y.
On sale at Town Hall Box Office, 113 West 43rd Street, two weeks in advance of concert.
For mail orders please enclose stamped addressed envelope.

COLUMBIA ARTISTS MANAGEMENT, INC.
111 West 57th Street   New York 19, New York
Recital Management: Anne J. O'Donnell, Manager

THE SUPERIOR PRINTING Co., N. Y.

Program for Town Hall recital, March 3, 1960

income from this position was supplemented by a class that I taught at the New School. I had proposed a course in aesthetics that extracted ideas about music and art that spanned a period from the ancient Greek philosophers to William James, Henri Bergson, and George Santayana. The hours that I had spent in reading the Harvard Classics series in Miss Lopez's house prompted me to embark upon this exploration.

Howard Hanson disliked dodecaphonic music. There were no courses offered in the use of this technique or any analysis of compositions representative of the second Viennese School. It mattered little to him that Eastman was mired in his taste. He had fostered an educational gap.

I had formed my own opinion about certain works in this style, which I studied without the benefit of any instruction.

The first and only used LP that I have ever bought was a recording of the Berg Violin Concerto played by Louis Krasner. The condition of the LP was suspect. Steel or cactus needles sharpened were the primitive conveyances used to extract the already deficient sound from the grooves of the LP. But I knew that there was something important in the music that could be revealed. When I heard a performance in Paris by the violinist Christian Ferras, it conveyed the transparency essential to comprehending this concerto.

Dodecaphony was acclaimed as the music of the avant-garde. But I was cognizant of the freedom that some composers indulged in while professing to use this technique. I decided to compose a strict, serial work for piano.

Spatials is a set of six variations called variants, derived from a theme called "Statement" that I composed in 1961. In the first two measures, the first twelve tones appear arpeggiated over three octaves. Each of the variants has a distinct character. The entire range of the piano is explored, often with great rapidity. The title of the work refers to the concept of dimensionality and disposition. The athleticism required of the pianist makes the Webern Variations for Piano seem staid and static by comparison. I had concluded that the only effective, strict use of twelve-tone technique would necessarily be a short work. Extended repetitions of the same notes, regardless of their selectivity from the matrix, result in a constricting sameness. (Modulation was a remarkable historical discovery.)

The first performance of *Spatials* was at Brandeis University in 1965. Arthur Berger of the music faculty remarked afterward that he wished that the variations were longer. He wasn't aware that their length had been predetermined. The brevity of *Spatials* requires a concentrated effort from a pianist. The short span of its duration does not permit the listener's attention to wander.

SMITH COLLEGE

Walter Hautzig, a close friend who for years jokingly reminded me that I had loaned him my white full dress vest for his successful Town Hall recital debut in 1944, informed me about a vacancy in the piano department at Smith College in Massachusetts. I applied for the position. After my audition there, I was sent a contract to teach piano and theory for the following academic year. I was accorded the rank of instructor despite the fact that I had a doctoral degree. Edwin London, hired as an assistant professor, was the only teacher other than me with a doctorate in the music department.

A few weeks later another letter inquired about my availability for the second semester of the 1960–1961 academic year. Complaints about an aging piano instructor who expressed her displeasure with her students by rapping them on their hands with a ruler had escalated. There was also a promising piano student who wanted to play a recital in her sophomore year. Joan Panetti was a perky, ambitious student with good facility, but insufficiently developed musically or technically at her age to embark upon a concert career.

Amherst College, located seven miles east of Northampton, had a music department that, like Harvard University, did not offer instrumental music instruction. I taught several men who came over to Smith to study piano. Their musical sensibilities and curiosity enabled them to give performances that had a stronger profile than those by the women students at Smith. Nevertheless, these women were diligent in their preparation, well motivated, very cooperative, and among the best students that I have taught. Elizabeth Carley (married name), who played a fine senior recital, has continued to communicate with me for over forty years.

Commuting to Northampton, Massachusetts, required the purchase of another car. (I had sold my DeSoto before going to Paris.) Gabriel Banat, a friend of Walter Hautzig, taught violin at Smith while maintaining his apartment in New York. Gabby generously loaned me his car for a trip from New Jersey to Northampton before I purchased another automobile. When Gabby refused to move to Northampton to continue his teaching at Smith, his contract was not renewed.

The music department at Smith was enamored of their chamber music concerts on which the same members of the faculty performed several times a year. When I mentioned in a casual conversation my willingness to play two recitals during my first year, some members of the faculty ostensibly recoiled at the prospect that there might be a prima donna in their midst. I sensed that this suggestion was not being received with approbation. But I made a habit of playing a solo piano recital every fall after John Duke's annual appearance. After forty years in the music department, his colleagues were not going to be critical of piano playing that never rose above the level of a dilettante.

Smith College was one of the colleges in the area that had a stake in Valley Music. It was a small company that published music of composers on the faculties of colleges in the area. This company published my first work, "Gloria in Memoriam," in 1963 for women's voices.

In the same year, I went to England to play another recital in Wigmore Hall in London. The trip was sponsored by Mrs. Efrem Zimbalist, who donated money for my expenses.

I also went to Paris to see Mlle. Boulanger for the last time. The principal work on the program in London was the Chopin Piano Sonata in B Minor. When I had returned home, I received a letter stating that I had been awarded an honorary membership in the Chopin Society there.

The *Grecourt Review* was an undergraduate publication at Smith College. Having learned that faculty members had submitted articles to it, I sent the editor several poems, "Must Hope Give Way to Doubt," "Morning Vigil," "It Is Clear That We Must End This," and "Rise from Your Curled Position." These were personal reflections about events in my life. I was pleased that three of these poems were published.

PUBLISHERS

I began to make a greater effort to get more of my music in print. I would drive down to New York periodically to meet editors of several publishing firms. The *Address for Orchestra* was published by MCA, and the Sonata for Violin and Piano, composed in Paris and now designated as my first sonata for these two instruments, was published by Associated Music

GEORGE WALKER, Pianist

WASHINGTON, D. C.

Great musical performers, as everybody knows, are very rare birds. What makes them great, above all else, is an intensely personal, yet faithful approach to the music at hand. A personality vivid enough, that is, to be able to infuse even the best-known music with the one ingredient that composers cannot get down on paper: The recreative spark of the performer . . .

Well, George Walker, who gave a piano recital at the National Gallery last night, has this recreative spark. And he's got enough technique to give brilliant accounts of such challenges as Chopin's F minor Fantasy and Liszt's Funerailles. Moreover, he is astonishingly sensitive to dynamic shading and has at his finger tips every kind of nuance you've ever heard of. . . The effect was dazzling.

(Washington Post)

NEW YORK, N. Y.

Throughout the evening, the interpretations were animated by knowledge and musicianship. His best playing came in the "Funerailles". This was a powerful conception, and one also in fine technical order. Mr. Walker's octaves rang forth unfalteringly, and he conveyed a strong idiomatic feeling for the music. His forte would appear to be in such large-scale works as this.

(Harold Schonberg, New York Times)

ROCHESTER, NEW YORK

A masterly performance of the Brahms 2nd concerto for piano and orchestra! . . . Mr. Walker set forth the piano core of the work with the right intellectual approach, coupled with a dazzling technical performance that realized the larger emotional context.

(Times-Union)

MILAN, ITALY

The pianist, George Walker, who was presented last evening at the Conservatory, is an artist who possesses an indisputable musical talent and interpretative finesse, and who has at his command an excellent technique. He has all the valid requisites for becoming as famous in Europe as he has in the United States.

(L'Italia)

FRANKFURT, GERMANY

George Walker's success in the auditorium of the university was great. There were many encores.

(Frankfurter Neue Presse)

NOW BOOKING

Back of a concert brochure

Publishers. Galaxy Music produced an autographed copy of my Piano Sonata no. 2. Later it was engraved by Associated Music, which also published a choral work, "Stars."

The *New York Times* used to print poems each week in a column on the left side of the second page in the Book Review section. After reading a poem entitled "Stars" by Susan A. Keeney, I felt that I could make a setting of it for a chorus SATB (soprano, alto, tenor, and bass). In 1969, I asked the choral director at the University of Colorado in Boulder, where I taught for a year after leaving Smith College, if he would include "Stars" on a program that his choir was preparing. When he agreed to include it on a program, I set up my portable Ampex PR-10 recorder, which had replaced the mono Ampex 350 recorder that I had in Northampton, to tape the concert. The PR-10 was a stereo tape deck. Since I only had one Neumann U-47 microphone, the sound was mono. But I wanted to have my own recording of "Stars." Sometime afterward, an engineer recorded the entire program for a noncommercial LP for the music department in Boulder.

Associated Music Publishers had agreed to publish "Stars" in 1968. But I had to get permission from the author to use the text. It required some sleuthing to locate Susan A. Keeney. I finally found the name "Keeney" in a Philadelphia telephone directory. When I called the telephone number, a lady answered. I told her that I was trying to find Ms. Keeney in order to obtain her permission to use the poem in the publication of my choral setting. The lady said that she was the sister of Susan A. Keeney. She added, "I know that my sister in heaven would approve of this." I sent her a cassette copy of my recording of the choral work. "Stars" is one of three works that are dedicated to my sister. The other two works are my *Prelude and Caprice* and *Guido's Hand* for piano.

ARTIST COLONIES

In the summer of 1966, I was invited to attend a reading session at the Composers Conference in Bennington, Vermont, after submitting a work to a jury that selected the composers. Two songs were sung at a concert there and Antifonys for Seven Winds, Percussion, and Double String Quartet (the work that garnered the fellowship covering my room and board) was read. The performances typified those generally given to contemporary music. The talented hired hands were quick study readers who had no time to polish anything.

In 1967 when I received a MacDowell Colony Fellowship, I had just begun work on my Second String Quartet. I drove to Peterboro, New Hampshire, in my green Peugeot sedan and was assigned a quaint studio with a piano after spending one night in Colony Hall. I was eager to write as much as I could during the weeks that I was there. Continuing what I had begun at home was surprisingly troublesome. I would divert my attention from this mental block by bringing in more firewood from the porch to watch the flames lick the logs in the fireplace. The period between the cafeteria-style breakfast and lunch delivered in a basket and left on the porch seemed overly long. It didn't help to walk around the area surrounding the studio. I tried to force myself to write something before dinner in Colony Hall. But I resisted the idea of starting a new work.

Dinner at the colony always provided a pleasant atmosphere. Artists and composers mingled afterward to talk about everything except what they were working on. An informative conversation with Gordon Binkerd enlightened me about the differences between the operations of ASCAP (American Society of Composers, Authors and Publishers) and BMI (Broadcast Music, Inc.). Gail Kubik explained the intricacies of composing for film to me. I saw Ed London from Smith College. He was surprised to see me at the colony. We did not speak, except for a greeting, about our common past.

David del Tredici and his Gedalge (French fugue text) were inseparable. He was hired to teach fugue at Harvard without having much knowledge about the subject. He engaged Stefan Wolpe, who appeared to be ill, in small talk at mealtime. Barbara Kolb effused approbation on the use of set (twelve tone) technique that she had adopted.

A cement tennis court with a barely serviceable net was located about a quarter of a mile off the main road leading from Colony Hall. I played on it a couple of times with some of the inmates who were hardly more than neophytes. Tennis on this level was not an enticing activity.

Walking on the same road lead to the town of Peterboro. The shops would have been more interesting to me if I had money for souvenirs.

Forcing myself to make the effort to produce something before leaving this lovely woodland environment that should have been conducive to achieving satisfactory results was a mistake. When I returned to Northampton and reviewed what I had accomplished, much of what I had written was disclaimed. A major revision was necessary to make the first movement acceptable.

The concept of creating arching soloistic lines unhampered by bar lines demanded precise pitch relationships to attain the melodic shape that I sought. The intertwining of these lines in all four parts of the string quartet was my objective. The desired effect would be an improvisatory quality with coincidental harmonic relationships.

The first movement of the string quartet was designed to be the most radical. The second movement (A–B–A) was conceived as a skittish scherzo. The B section, corresponding to a trio in the classical minuet-scherzo form, is lyrical. A transitional passage leads to the return of the A section. The third movement begins with a single note, B, and expands with double stops amid punctuating pizzicati for nine measures to complete the phrase. The introduction to the fourth movement is connected to a four-voice fugue via an ascending line that begins in the cello. The head of the fugue subject is stated in the viola before the entire subject appears in the second violin part.

I returned to the MacDowell Colony in 1968 and made a string orchestra version of Antiphonys for Seven Winds, Percussion, and Double String Quartet.

SMITH COLLEGE PROJECTS

Walter Hautzig, who had been teaching piano at the Peabody Conservatory in Baltimore, asked me if I knew any establishment in New England that would be interested in hosting a summer school for Peabody students. I made an appointment with Thomas Mendenhall, the president of Smith College, to present a proposal that would utilize the buildings on the campus during the summer. When the agreement was reached with Peabody, the first year of several summer programs at Smith was instituted in 1967. For the inaugural concert I played a recital with the cellist, Paul Olefsky, that included my Cello Sonata.

I received a visit at Smith from Joel Spielgelman, a composer and conductor, who had been studying composition in Paris when I was there in 1957–1958. He was a member of the composition faculty at Brandeis University in Waltham, Massachusetts. We discussed the possibility of arranging two concerts of contemporary music. The composers at Smith would present a program at Brandeis and the composers at Brandeis would give a concert at Smith. The collaboration was a failure in terms of audience support. At Brandeis, the only persons present besides the composers were their wives. I still find it hilarious in recalling Joel's remark about his colleagues when he said that "they fight like cats and dogs."

In order to keep up with other colleges that had created electronic labs, the Music Department at Smith decided to make a small room available for the composers who were interested in this medium. I volunteered to recommend the necessary components for a rudimentary audio system. After coming to Smith, I had been using various Ampex tape recorders and other ancillary equipment purchased from audio stores in New York City. I taped FM broadcasts and preconcert rehearsals for the piano recitals that I played. My knowledge about audio had increased considerably. I was able to use it years later in the production of my own CDs.

PROMOTION

I had been promoted at Smith from the lowly rank of instructor to assistant professor. Three years later I was eligible for a promotion to associate professor. The chairman of the Music Department, Vernon Gotwals, sent me a brief note in 1967 at the conclusion of the academic year. The department had decided to terminate me after the following year. I was shocked. My theory students had surpassed those of the former chairman of the Music Department, Gertrude Smith, who had hired me. In the joint exams that we gave, my students received more than twice as many As in the grading that we did together. My piano students were the best performers in the department. My piano recitals attracted many professors from other departments and persons in the town who admired my playing.

The most active private piano teacher in Northampton was Mrs. Warren, a lovely lady who entrusted me to teach her three most advanced students. Mariola was the pride of her life. When I moved to Montclair, New Jersey, she continued her lessons with me. Her mother would drive her to New Jersey twice a month. Her former teacher paid for her lessons. When Mariola finished high school, she received a scholarship to the Eastman School of Music.

Two young men, Mike and Charles, had piano lessons with me on Saturdays when I was at Smith. Before they graduated from high school, I arranged for them to give a joint recital in Sage Hall at Smith College. One of them went on to Harvard University.

The Smith College Music Department had no procedure for evaluating a professor's teaching. One visit was made to my theory class by Phillip Keppler, a southerner with whom I had no contact as a colleague. He taught music history and was a friend of Gotwals. Several months later he died from cirrhosis of the liver.

A majority of the tenured professors in the Music Department— the well-entrenched spinsters as well as Robert Miller, a mediocre pianist; John Duke; and Philip Nagele, a violinist at the time—had no intention of breaking the existing precedent of the college by giving an associate professorship and tenure to a black person. The quality of performance and teaching that I brought to a rather run-of-the-mill department was ignored.

As with many discriminatory decisions, little thought was given to potential repercussions. Gotwals took the brunt of the criticsm. Letters that poured in from all of my piano students (except for Panetti), outrage expressed by faculty members in other departments, and the support of persons in the town of Northampton resulted in the revoking of the decision. In officially informing me of this, President Tom Mendenhall was less than gracious in begrudging the reversal. I became the first black professor to receive tenure at Smith College.

In 1968, when the country was fermenting with civil rights demonstrations, I wrote to Mendenhall about the hiring of domestic workers at Smith College. A well-poised black woman living in nearby Springfield, Massachusetts, had complained to me that she had applied several times for a job at Smith College. No one at Smith would offer her work. There were no minorities represented in maintenance positions there. Mendenhall never replied to my letter.

I was invited to speak during the Sunday morning service of a Protestant Church in Amherst, Massachusetts. In the brief talk that I gave, I mentioned the discrimination that Mohammed Ali was subjected to when he refused to join the armed services in World War II. Although I was appalled by the "rope a dope" defense that contributed to his physical deterioration, his conscientious objection to fighting that was based on his religious beliefs should never have resulted in the temporary loss of his heavyweight boxing title. After the service only one person spoke to me about my talk. He was the minister who had invited me.

ORCHESTRAL PERFORMANCES

In 1968 the New World Symphony, an interracial orchestra in New York City, expressed interest in performing my *Address for Orchestra* in Avery Fisher Hall. When I met the conductor, Benjamin Steinberg, one of the cofounders of the ensemble, he told me that he only wanted to play the first and third movements of the work. He asserted that he would "lose his audience" if the second movement was played.

The flyer for the concert stated that the *Address for Orchestra* had been commissioned. This was blatantly false as I had already composed the music before I met Steinberg. The excision of the second movement meant that the score was truncated. The miserable concert performance was due to poor rehearsal techniques and to the incompetence of the conductor.

One of the most significant events in the development of my career as a composer also occurred in 1968. I received a letter from Paul Freeman, who was an undergraduate at the Eastman School of Music when I was completing my doctoral degree. We had been in the same conducting class of Paul White. In the form letter was a request for scores that could be read by the Atlanta Symphony in a symposium sponsored by the Rockefeller Foundation. Spelman College was the site for this event.

The Rockefeller Foundation had been subsidizing readings of orchestral music for several years. But this was the first time that black composers had been invited to participate in these sessions. It also marked the first time that a group of black composers had been assembled to hear their music. The problems associated with getting performances of their scores were among the principal topics discussed.

At the conclusion of the reading sessions conducted by Freeman, Robert Shaw, conductor of the Atlanta Symphony, and Freeman chose several works that were performed in a concert at Spelman College. The black composers attending the symposium were Ulysses Kay, T. J. An-

derson, and myself. Also represented in the reading sessions were Olly
Wilson and Adolphus Hailstork, who was in Germany. The third movement of my *Address for Orchestra* concluded the concert.

In an article in *Newsweek* magazine, Robert Shaw lauded the quality
of the music and the contribution that black composers have made to classical music whilst being virtually unknown. There were additional sympo-
sia in Baltimore and Minneapolis in which Paul Freeman was again the
conductor. In Baltimore, my Variations for Orchestra were performed.

All of the composers in Atlanta stayed in a modest motel that did
not serve meals. One evening I left my room at dinnertime to take the
elevator to the small lobby. Someone at the desk said that there was a
meeting of the Southern Christian Conference taking place in a room
on that level. The heavy oak door of the room had a rectangular glass
window about six feet from its base. I pressed my face close to the glass.
At that moment I saw one of the ministers move to embrace Dr. Martin
Luther King. The meeting had concluded. The door opened suddenly
as I moved away from it. This was the only time that I had glimpsed
this courageous but flawed man.

SUMMER FESTIVAL

In the summer of 1968, Paul Olefsky, the cellist who was again on the
summer faculty of the Peabody Institute, organized a music festival at
the University of Massachusetts. He formed a quartet that played my
Second String Quartet and the Beethoven String Quartet op. 95 on the
same concert. I was the pianist in Schumann's Piano Quintet.

In September Olefsky arranged three concerts in Town Hall, New
York, using the works that he had programmed in Amherst and adding
the Bach Brandenburg Concerto no. 5 and the string orchestra version
of my Antifonys for Chamber Orchestra. The *New York Times* praised
the unique quality of the Second String Quartet that was played on
one of the programs with the op. 95 of Beethoven. The first violinist
in the string quartet, William Steck, became the concertmaster of the
National Symphony in Washington, DC, after having played in the
Cleveland Orchestra under George Szell.

TOWN HALL HEARS NEW ENGLANDERS

Festival Chamber Players Offer Strong Program

By RAYMOND ERICSON

A bit of the summer musical scene spilled over into Town Hall last night. The New England Festival Chamber Players, sponsored by the University of Massachusetts at Amherst last month in a new series of concerts, gathered up their instruments and music and came to town to show New Yorkers what they had been up to.

The series put emphasis on the music of composers teaching at schools in the Amherst area, and last night the one so honored was George Walker, who is on the Smith College faculty. Besides being represented by a creative work, he appeared as a pianist with a string quartet drawn from the larger ensemble.

Tomorow night the full group will give a program in Town Hall, playing another piece by Mr. Walker and one by Philip Bezanson of the University of Massachusetts faculty.

The string quartet was made up of William Steck and Matitiahu Braun, violinists; Sally Trembly, violist, and Paul Olefsky, cellist and guiding spirit of the Festival Chamber Players. The program included Beethoven's Quartet in F minor (Op. 95), Mr. Walker's String Quartet (1968) and Schumann's Piano Quintet in E flat.

Strong Competition

The Beethoven, with its extraordinarily bold shifts in key, and the Schumann, with its wonderful lyricism and color, are familiar masterpieces. What was gratifying was the fact that the Walker quartet held up very well between two such strong works. The 41-year-old composer uses serial techniques in a straightforward, highly expressive manner, and he treats the instruments traditionally. The writing is delicate, clear-textured and fluid, sensitive to the need for dramatic phrases as contrast and highlight. For all its transparency, the music has admirable momentum, fostered less by strong rhythms than by the constant variation in instrumental color.

The performances were of a high order, despite the fact that details of phrasing and balance could be faulted. Mr. Walker, who appeared as a recitalist here as a young man, brought an authoritative manner to the Schumann that seemed to make his colleagues add fervor to their playing. For a concert so early in the new season, this one had more rewards than might have been expected.

New York Times *article on New England Festival, 1968*

UNIVERSITY OF COLORADO

I took a leave of absence from Smith College after receiving tenure there. I had received an invitation from David Burge, a pianist whom I had known at Eastman, to come to the University of Colorado (Boulder) in 1968 as a visiting professor for a year. He had taken a sabbatical leave. I taught piano and a course in piano literature. I was also able to complete a three-movement symphony that was read with considerable difficulty by the University Orchestra. The first and third movements were abandoned a few years later. The second movement was retained and incorporated with modifications in my Serenata for Chamber Orchestra.

The rather large music department was more ambitious than capable in developing a first-rate undergraduate program. Some of the technical requirements for pianists instituted by the chairman of the piano department were beyond the pale. But the students whom I taught were talented and congenial.

MOVE TO NEW JERSEY

In the spring of 1969, a friend, Alfred Mann, the musicologist known for his translation from the German of Fux's *Gradus ad Parnassum*, proposed my name to the chairmen of the Rutgers University music departments in both New Brunswick and Newark for a faculty position. Alfred had been a student of Scalero at Curtis before I came to Curtis. I accepted the offer of a full professorship from the Newark campus rather than a job from the New Brunswick campus because I wanted to be closer to New York. Moreover, I had heard that the tenured professors at the New Brunswick campus were a contentious lot. Their doctoral program was rigid and unduly protracted.

I resigned my position as an associate professor at Smith College, which, as one of the Seven Sisters, paid miserly salaries. I had applied for a Guggenheim Fellowship in composition in the fall of 1968. The application that I submitted was successful. I received the first of two awards from this foundation in the spring of 1969.

I was fortunate in obtaining the assistance of a fair-minded realtor, Howard Johnson, in finding a house in Montclair, New Jersey. After showing me several houses that did not meet my needs, he allowed me to search the files in his office for potentially satisfactory homes in my price range. I had heard about Montclair from Dr. Bertram Phillips, whose former wife had lived there. The town is known for its diverse population. However, busing was mandated in 1969, the year that I arrived, to offset segregation in the public schools. The location of the majority of the black population in the southern end of the town had created this problem. There were only a few black families living in Upper Montclair.

The division of the town into two separate postal zones can be misleading for those who assume that Upper Montclair is the more desirable location. The wealthiest homes are in Montclair, not Upper Montclair. The public schools in Montclair were considered to be good. But there was overcrowding in some grades and some of the teachers in the high school were viewed as biased. It was asserted that black students were less likely to get into the advanced placement courses. Some of the grade school teachers were inexperienced.

The house that I purchased was on Grove Street, a busy corridor connecting several towns in a north-south direction. Noisy trucks, ambulances, police cars, and fire engines constantly polluted the air. In converting a dining room into a music room in my house, the extraneous sounds that penetrated the living room were substantially reduced. To make recordings in the music room it was necessary to wait until late evening when the traffic outside had diminished. The flight paths of planes from Newark Airport created more of the same problem at night.

Montclair has long been considered a highly desirable town for families seeking to escape from claustrophobic locations in Manhattan and the perils of Brooklyn, New York. But it has become obscenely inflationary with appallingly high property taxes, water bills, sewer bills, and alarm system taxes. The increase in and replication of ethnic restaurants and the diversification of its population cannot offset the oppressive demands of the town government. The *Montclair Times*, formerly owned by Republican zealots, is attuned to the concerns of the Democratic majority in the town. But like most newspapers, its pointed focus is ineffectual in slowing down the changing character of this residential location.

RUTGERS UNIVERSITY

It was a rather easy commute from Montclair to the Rutgers University Campus in Newark. Parking was more of a problem. The Music Department was founded by Alfred Mann. A renovated stable contained a few rooms used for class instruction. After my first year at Rutgers, the Music Department was moved to a warehouse donated to the university by the Prudential Insurance Company. The Music Department occupied the second floor. There was no concert hall. Funds were allocated by the university for the purchase of six new Steinway B pianos. My studio had two of these instruments.

There was some discussion in the early 1970s about constructing a building for all of the arts. With the increased enrollment of students determined to insure their financial future, accounting courses were in great demand. There was no administrative leadership in the university to promote the creation of a performing arts center on the campus. When the Performing Arts Center in Newark was being planned, it was easy for some professors to rationalize that a university arts center would be unnecessary. The idea was inconspicuously sacked. It may never have sufficiently impressed these persons that impoverished students would not be able to afford the prices for events in this venue.

There was no chapel on the Newark campus and no appropriate auditorium for concerts. Convocations were held in the gym. The Music Department was granted permission to leave one of the Steinway B pianos in a room on the top floor of the Newark Public Library that was close to the campus. This was the location of the annual piano recitals that I gave.

For my first year at Rutgers (1969) I taught piano, keyboard harmony, and second-year theory. Several students were the first persons in their family to attend a college. I felt a strong responsibility to give them what I had absorbed from my experiences. Their musical backgrounds were quite limited. But they worked conscientiously at their assignments. Providing them with the training and the perspective that would enable them to compete with students from better equipped institutions was my objective.

At a reception given by Rutgers University for retiring professors, I spoke about the satisfaction that I felt in having taught twelve different courses. Although many persons had concluded that I was no longer playing concerts, I played a solo piano recital every year of my tenure at Rutgers.

Composing, Performing, and Publishing

1970s

$\mathscr{I}$n the course of a conversation with Howard Klein of the Rockefeller Foundation in New York, I was offered a fellowship to the foundation's Bellagio Center in Italy. This idyllic retreat on Lake Como was an ideal location for me to compose my Variations for Orchestra in 1971. I had been fascinated by a new approach to variation techniques. In this work there is no identifiable theme. Each variation has its own motivic set. Within some of the variations is a brief recurrence of material present in an earlier variation. There is a conscious exploration of orchestral color that separates one variation from another with contrasts in rhythmic patterns.

Natalie Hinderas was a child prodigy who played the Grieg Piano Concerto with the Cleveland Women's Orchestra when she was twelve years old. I heard her play the concerto in Finney Chapel when I was a junior at Oberlin. She lived with her grandmother in Oberlin. When I returned to Oberlin to work on my master's degree in the summer of 1942, she invited my sister and me to visit her. After I told her that I was learning the Beethoven Concerto no. 1, she managed to sight-read some of the second piano part of the third movement that I played for her. Natalie decided to enter the Oberlin Conservatory after she finished high school and chose to study with my former teacher, David Moyer.

Both she and my sister, Frances, became staunch advocates of piano music by black composers. In 1971 Natalie asked me to come to a recording session of works by Thomas Kerr, Arthur Cunningham, Stephen Chambers (Talib Rasul Hakim), Hale Smith, and others that had been arranged by Desto Records. The room was in a loft around

Seventy-fifth Street and Broadway in New York. My Piano Sonata no. 1 was the major work that she recorded. Horace Grinnell, president of Desto Records, was the engineer who taped and edited the sonata. The boxed set of piano works by black composers became the first of its kind to be issued commercially.

I received a letter from the *Music Educators Journal* requesting me to review a new book by Dr. Eileen Southern entitled *The Music of Black Americans*. It had just been published by W. W. Norton in 1971. I was immediately impressed by the wide range of material that was discussed in this publication and the accuracy of the details that had been uncovered. It was the first book of significance and depth on this subject. I may have been the first person to have reviewed it.

In 1974 Columbia Records released the first recordings in their Black Composers series. My Concerto for Trombone and Orchestra was included in volume 3, the *Lyric for Strings* in volume 7, and the Piano Concerto in volume 9. This series received outstanding reviews. It created an awareness by the white press of black composers from the eighteenth century to the twentieth century. But Columbia Records failed to take full advantage of the impact made by these recordings. Two years after being issued, they could only be found in discount stores. An important review of the Black Composers series was scheduled to appear in the *New York Times*. When Carman Moore, a black composer, was dilatory in preparing it, I spoke to Howard Klein who agreed to write a review of it. The College Music Society reissued the series in 1987 with a grant from the Ford Foundation.

General Music Publishing Company

In a conversation that I had with Horace Grinnell, I mentioned that I wanted to have more of my music published. He suggested that I contact Paul Kapp, who had cofounded General Music Publishing Company.

The first offices of General Music were in Manhattan. I climbed the dirty, narrow steps of several floors with walls painted yellow to reach Paul Kapp's headquarters. In greeting me, he wasted no time in asking what I would like to have published. I told him, "My songs." He said, "What else"? I replied, "My Piano Sonata no. 1." After several years of trying to convince Galaxy Music, Associated Music, and MCA to publish more of my works, I was astonished to have a verbal agreement for several works made so easily.

Paul Kapp was an extraordinarily devoted publisher of music by American composers. Before deciding to concentrate on publishing as his principal activity, he told me that he had managed a black male vocal quartet. He had published "I Left My Heart in San Francisco" before it became Tony Bennett's signature song. Paul also controlled the performance rights for "The Singing Nun." Royalties from these two songs and his social security provided him with sufficient income to manage his publishing company. He also created a recording company called Serenus Records.

After I met Paul Kapp, he moved his firm to Dobbs Ferry, New York. Approximately fifty of my works were published before his death in 1984. He never asked me for a cent to have my music engraved nor did he charge me to produce LPs of my chamber and orchestral works that he paid to be recorded. I watched him in his office as he designed with a compass a monogram using my initials for the cover of one LP recording. My Variations for Orchestra were recorded in London after its premiere by the New Philharmonia Orchestra on a program conducted by Paul Freeman. An errant comment by an English critic likened the work to the Variations of Schoenberg.

Paul sent my Cello Sonata to Czechoslovakia to be engraved. Five months later he received a package that contained only the piano part and the cello part, not the score. He told me that he would not make a complaint about this with the engraving company in Czechoslovakia because he knew that the person who made the mistake would be fired by his communist superiors. Paul paid another copyist in New York to make the score.

On another LP that I shared with Meyer Kupferman, Antifonys for Chamber Orchestra was recorded by the Royal Philharmonic Orchestra. The principal cellist of the Detroit Symphony, Italo Babini, and I recorded my Sonata for Cello and Piano in a studio in lower Manhattan.

Meyer Kupferman was the first composer of contemporary classical music to be published by Paul Kapp. For several years Meyer received a stipend from General Music.

Paul was a collector of rare books. He liked to photograph pictures from these books to place on the covers of the music that he published. He would also hire commercial artists to draw designs for the covers of sheet music. He disliked what he called the "Germanic" influence in the sober, unimaginative lettering used on covers from the major music publishing houses.

Paul had a strained relationship with his son, Richard. Dick Kapp's chamber orchestra had made several very successful recordings, beginning with *The Greatest Hits of 1970* for Columbia Records. But Paul's fondness for my *Lyric for Strings* was strong enough to overcome his reluctance to urge his son to perform it. When Dick Kapp took the Philharmonia Virtuosi to Japan for a tour, he included my string orchestra work on his programs.

After Paul's death, Dick inherited the operations of the publishing company. His primary interest, however, was in conducting the Philharmonia Virtuosi of New York, the chamber ensemble that he founded.

David Ensemble

Warren Wilson, a pianist and conductor who had formed a chamber music group called the David Ensemble, contacted me about composing a work for piano four hands and clarinet. My first reaction to the inquiry was an admission that this request was puzzling. I had composed a work for piano and clarinet called *Perimeters* in 1963, and I was willing to write another work for a duo. Warren insisted that he wanted a four-hand work for an Alice Tully Recital Hall program on which the clarinetist, Richard Stoltzman, would be playing. A friend of Warren, an English pianist, was also an integral member of the David Ensemble. The commission for *Five Fancies for Clarinet and Piano Four Hands* was the first in my career as a composer that paid me money. The premiere was given in April of 1975. *Five Fancies* is probably the only existent work for this repertoire. It is a set of variations on five notes.

New Positions

Richard Goldman, director of the Peabody Institute of Johns Hopkins University, offered me a contract to teach piano and composition to a few students in 1975. I had just become the chairman of the Music Department at Rutgers at that time. Two of my four undergraduate students, a pianist and a composition major, received the top awards at Peabody before I left in 1978. Michael Coonrod, a doctor-of-musical-arts student in piano, became an important member of the faculty at the Interlochen Arts Academy.

In the same year (1975), the University of Delaware awarded me their first Minority Chair, a professorship for one year. I spent a great deal of time commuting to Baltimore and Delaware by train and by car from my home in Montclair, New Jersey, over a period of three years. During that time I was also busy composing.

Lincoln Center Events

A series of concerts of music by black composers was presented in New York in 1977. Working with AAMOA (the African-American Music Opportunities Association), Leon Thompson, director of educational activities for the New York Philharmonic, and I fashioned programs involving the New York Philharmonic. My *Lyric for Strings* and my Piano Concerto were performed in Avery Fisher Hall, Lincoln Center, on one of the orchestral programs.

The low-keyed reviews that appeared in the New York newspapers were indicative of a lack of comprehension of the importance of these events. The sterling performance of Sanford Allen in the New York premiere of a superb violin concerto by Roque Cordero was ignored, as was the powerful playing of Natalie Hinderas in my Piano Concerto. Harold Schonberg directed most of his skewed comments to the quality of Allen's Stradivari. Critics for newspapers in other cities were decidedly more enthusiastic about this concert by the New York Philharmonic.

One of the unusual aspects of my Piano Concerto occurs in the second movement. A familiar song by Duke Ellington is used as the entire movement and is quoted in augmentation. It is unrecognizable in this setting. The third movement begins as a full-fledged fugue, complete with counter subject. The concerto was not composed as a memorial to Ellington as some musicologists have presumed. But I did want it to have a connection to another Washingtonian working in a different milieu. Another concert in the Black Composers event was a piano recital on which Leon Bates played my Piano Sonata no. 1.

Commissions

Preceding the celebration of the bicentennial of this country in 1976, I received three commissions. My Piano Sonata no. 3 was commissioned by the Washington Performing Arts Society. The premiere was given by Leon Bates at the Kennedy Center for the Performing Arts. Leon recorded the sonata for Desto Records on an LP with music by MacDowell and Barber. *Music for Brass (Sacred and Profane)* was commissioned by the Hans Kindler Foundation.

A few months after my orchestral debut with the Philadelphia Orchestra in 1945, I learned that Hans Kindler, the conductor of the National Symphony in Washington, would be coming to Curtis to audition some students for positions in his orchestra. I asked Jane Hill if I could play for him. The outcome of the audition duplicated one that I had with Vladimir Golschmann, conductor of the Saint Louis Symphony. Neither of these persons was willing to discuss an engagement for me after I had finished playing. Both were ensconced in a discriminatory musical environment. Receiving a commission from a foundation named after a conductor who had shown no interest in me seemed ironic.

Kindler, a Dutch cellist who played in the Philadelphia Orchestra, had founded the National Symphony. As a conductor, he commanded little respect from members of the National Symphony. The home of the National Symphony was the infamous Constitution Hall.

I spoke with Robert Nagel about the commission that I had been offered by the Hans Kindler Foundation. Nagel was a trumpet player in the New York Brass Quintet. He suggested, in the conversation that I had with him at Rutgers where he was an adjunct instructor, that a work for a brass quintet would have a celebratory quality in the bicentennial. I composed *Music for Brass (Sacred and Profane)* for his ensemble. The work has four movements, two of which are dancelike.

I did not hear a rehearsal of it before its premiere. I assumed that Nagel would prepare the score responsibly. My assumption was ill founded. The New York Brass Quintet failed to adequately rehearse the music. The performance in the Textile Museum in Washington, DC, was a sham. After the concert I went to the backstage area to talk to the ensemble. The entire quintet had left hastily and probably sheepishly. I have not seen any of them since that concert.

The four movements of *Music for Brass* consist of arrangements of two works originally composed for an organ service: hence the reference to "sacred." "Liebster Jesu, Wir Sind Hier," a chorale prelude, receives a treatment radically different from the prelude on the same hymn tune by J. S. Bach. A brief lyrical introduction that returns at the conclusion of the work frames the chorale. A canon is inserted in the middle. The chorale melody is stripped of the excessive ornamentation of the Bach setting. This is a very compact miniature.

The second organ work, *Invokation* (not Invocation), is more complex. A double fugue is preceded by an imposing introduction that also returns to end the work. There are modal implications that hark back to the sixteenth-century music of the Catholic Church and techniques that anticipate those employed in the Protestant baroque form.

Two dancelike movements alternate with the "sacred" sections. Parts of both of these dance movements were composed in the 1960s. At that time a graduate student from England was writing her master's thesis at Smith College on the masques of Ben Jonson. She wanted some music for a lecture on the subject. I wrote several pieces for the no. 2 student string quartet in the Music Department after she told me that the no. 1 string quartet was too busy to work on anything new. The two dances used in *Music for Brass* were taken from that score. The second dance contains a quote from a popular standard, "Once in a While," which I heard at one of the "recs" in my freshman dormitory at Oberlin College.

I received a telephone call from Lorin Maazel, who wanted to discuss a commission for the Cleveland Orchestra. He suggested that I consider composing either a concerto for orchestra or a concerto for the principal cellist of the Cleveland Orchestra, Stephen Geber. After deciding to write a cello concerto, I applied for and received a second Rockefeller Foundation Fellowship to go to Bellagio, Italy. I spent three weeks creating a piano score of the concerto in the Villa Serbelloni.

Dialogus for Cello and Orchestra is a work in one movement with a duration of thirteen minutes. The solo part alternates between long lyrical lines and energetic virtuosic material. I orchestrated the concerto after I returned home. Figurations that occur in the orchestral part are suggestive of the outdoor environment surrounding the studio in which I worked. The chirping of birds and rustling of insects above the placid waters of Lake Como created a forestlike atmosphere.

Maazel's request for the piano score before the completion of the full score was most surprising, although Marin Alsop made a similar request recently. Most conductors prefer to wait for the finished score. The premiere of *Dialogus* on the subscription series of the Cleveland Orchestra was very successful. This compensated in part for the meager commission of two thousand dollars that I received. The orchestra was unwilling initially to pay my expenses to Cleveland to attend the performances for this bicentennial celebration in 1976. Geber received a rousing ovation. He remarked that it was the most difficult work that he had ever played. The clear, soprano-like quality of his cello was well suited to the high tessitura of his part.

The concert began with the Beethoven Symphony no. 1. Maazel fussed with the introduction of the first movement for at least twenty-five minutes, while imploring the orchestra to make it sound like "chamber music." If he had spent more time on the rest of the work, the performance of the symphony would not have been so ragged.

Baltimore Symphony

For several years I had considered composing a Mass using the traditional Latin text for the five parts of the Ordinary with a large orchestra, soloists, and chorus—an antidote to a work with the same title by Leonard Bernstein. The Baltimore Symphony agreed to perform it with the Morgan State College Choir conducted by Nathan Carter. I had received a grant from the National Endowment for the Arts to compose it. When I informed Sergiu Comissiona, the conductor of the Baltimore Symphony, that there were parts for four soloists—soprano, alto, tenor, and bass—he wanted members of the Morgan State Choir to sing them. I expressed my objection to this. There were already four solo parts for singers in the chorus. The major solo parts were intended to be sung by experienced professionals.

The administration of the Baltimore Symphony relented. I personally auditioned a group of singers in New York and made the selection for the four parts. The score requires an organ. Since the hall did not have one, a synthesizer was used instead. The Mass was given an impressive performance in 1977. The associate conductor of the Baltimore Symphony, Andrew Schenck, told Comissiona after the concert that "there was not a weak measure in the entire Mass."

Comissiona had programmed my *Address for Orchestra* a few years before the premiere of my Mass. Two days before the first performance in Baltimore, I received a call from him. He began by stating that Milstein, who was playing the Beethoven Violin Concerto on the concert, was a difficult person and that although he had played the work 250 times, he still insisted on an exorbitant amount of rehearsal. Comissiona said that he would not have sufficient time to prepare all three movements of my

Address. He wanted me to choose one movement that he could play. I chose the first movement because there had been numerous performances of the third movement. For these performances it was titled *Passacaglia*. After the concert Milstein appeared to be totally self-absorbed and uncommunicative. But his violin produced an exceptionally warm quality.

Piano Concerto

The National Endowment for the Arts awarded a grant to me for a piano concerto that would be played by Natalie Hinderas. The idea of having a work written for her was broached in a conversation that she had with Robert Shaw of the Atlanta Symphony. He had recommended me as an "obvious choice" to her. Natalie gave the official premiere with the Minneapolis Symphony in 1976. However, her former student, Horatio Miller, played one movement of the Piano Concerto with an orchestra in the Academy of Music in Philadelphia under James Fraser a few months earlier, in 1975. When Fraser beckoned to me to take a bow with him, I desperately, but unsuccessfully, tried to penetrate the milling chorus that blocked the opening to the stage. The next work on the program was the Beethoven Ninth Symphony. The composer of the Piano Concerto had been swallowed up in this mass of humanity.

After Natalie performed the Piano Concerto with the New York Philharmonic in its Celebration of Black Composers in 1977, there were other performances by the National Symphony in Washington, DC, with Skrowaczewski conducting, and by the Dallas Symphony, conducted by Eduardo Mata.

For the performance by the National Symphony in the Kennedy Center for the Performing Arts I was given a box seat. There were only two works on the program. My Piano Concerto preceded the Bruckner Fourth Symphony. While I was reading the program notes, two women entered the adjacent box. They began to chat. One of them asked about the husband of the other woman. The latter replied that her husband intended to remain in the men's room until the contemporary work was over.

The recording of the Piano Concerto that Natalie Hinderas made with the Detroit Symphony in the Black Composers series on an LP was reissued by Sony in a two-disk CD package with the Cordero Violin Concerto and Celebration by Adolphus Hailstork.

Distinguished Professorship

In 1976 after I had become the chairman of the Music Department at Rutgers, I was promoted to the position of professor II (distinguished professor). There had never been anyone in the arts in the entire Rutgers University system (five colleges) who had attained that rank.

Alfred Mann, who was on the graduate music faculty on the New Brunswick campus, taught one undergraduate course, counterpoint, on the Newark campus. My promotion inspired his department in New Brunswick to promote him to the position of distinguished professor. When Alfred decided to leave Rutgers before he was forced to retire, he accepted a teaching position at the Eastman School of Music. He told me that his promotion benefitted him in his salary negotiations with Eastman.

String Competition

The National Black Music Competition in 1979 attracted pianists and string players from every part of the country. When I was first informed about the competition, I contacted numerous persons to make them aware of this opportunity. I met with Dorothy Delay at Juilliard to discuss the requirements and to ask her support in soliciting black string players. She had been a transfer student at Oberlin College and had played a chamber music work on a program on which I played. But I did not know her at that time.

Winners of the auditions were assured of appearances with major symphony orchestras. Each contestant was required to perform a work by a black composer and compositions of their choice. Several of my works were played. Alison Deane, who received the first prize in the piano competition, played my *Spatials* and *Spektra* for piano. I was drafted to play the piano part of my Violin and Piano Sonata no. 1 on an hour's notice. Darwyn Apple, a violinist from the Saint Louis Symphony, did not have an accompanist.

Marcus Thompson, a violist, received an award in the string competition. A double bass player was also given a prize. This event was never repeated. It preceded the Sphinx Competition established by Aaron Dworkin by seventeen years.

An equally important and enterprising effort to encourage minority participation in classical music is the string program, Project Step, in Boston. It was cofounded twenty-five years ago by Bill Moyer, the son of

THE SUN, Sunday, June 14, 1981

Work by Rutgers composer to premiere at brass festival here

By Jack Dawson
Sun Staff Correspondent

Montclair, N.J.—George Walker does not know what he missed when he was growing up in Washington.

He didn't hear much jazz as a youngster. Instead he had to practice the piano every day—classical music yet. That did not leave much time for sports or girl friends, either.

All that work paid off, though, not only for George Walker, who went on to become a teacher, performer and composer of classical music, but for Baltimore audiences, who can hear the premiere of his "Music for Diverse Instruments" at 7:30 p.m. Thursday, June 25, at the Cross Keys Village Square in Baltimore.

The work was composed for the International Brass Quintet Festival at Cross Keys, which begins this week. The June 25 program will include American music performed by the Annapolis Brass Quintet, the resident ensemble of the festival, and the Festival Brass Ensemble.

The festival begins at 12:30 p.m. Tuesday with a performance by the Annapolis group and continues through July 11. As composer in residence, Walker will lecture on "Twentieth Century Composition" at 7:30 p.m. Tuesday, June 23, and a concert a seminar at 2:30 p.m. Wednesday, June 24, at the Cross Keys clubhouse.

If the June 25 presentation bears any resemblance to Mr. Walker's impromptu reading on his Steinway grand, audiences will find the piece thoughtful to the point of being haunting, with a sweeping rhythmic style.

The 58-year-old composer-pianist, a music educator at Rutgers University, was interviewed at his home in a quiet residential neighborhood of this New York City commuter town. He confessed humorously about the premiere.

"It's rhythmically complicated and the range is quite extreme for those instruments," he said. "I made the choice, perhaps because I was exposed to Stravinsky over Schoenberg or Webern."

Although he has composed more than 40 published pieces, as well as 8 or 10 large-scale orchestral works which remain unpublished, Dr. Walker said he is more concerned about quality than quantity of his life's work. "I'd prefer a few good pieces to a variety of good and bad," he said.

"My basic concern is not to repeat myself, which is always a danger for a composer," he added. "Inevitably there is some overlap, because your mind is still involved in certain technical aspects. The solution is whether to break off completely or expand on [the technical aspects] in your next composition."

Dr. Walker is more relaxed about writing now than formerly, mostly because he has found he can be creative at any time. "I used to keep a very disciplined schedule. I'd go to bed early because I thought it was important to be fresh in the morning," he said.

"I take a very different view of writing now, because I find my mind is working if I sit down at a table or the piano. The main thing is to allow sufficient time to complete my work, so I try to spend three or four hours every day.

"I do very little rewriting other than minute adjustments and refinements," he said. "But I'm always going back to pieces to see if I want to polish or upgrade them."

Dr. Walker's work is clearly tied to the more adventurous Twentieth Century composers, but retains basic elements of melody, harmony and rhythm.

"It is possible to be a contemporary composer without negating these basic elements," he said. "Some compositions may have more of a sense of fantasy or abstract shape; another may vary rhythms, but any form of creative endeavor you must be concerned with basic elements.

"It is possible to write something atonal that has melodic elements, but that is difficult to achieve," he added. "For instance, the Berg Violin Concerto is highly emotionally charged and has sufficient atonal elements to take it out of tonal music. But it also has attractive melodic

contours that for me make it a powerful and representative piece of Twentieth Century music.

Dr. Walker has never had any particular classical heroes—composers or performers—although he has been influenced by certain qualities of several artists and creators. "I've tended to relate to specific works or certain aspects of a composer at various times," he said.

George Walker, composer, pianist and teacher, and his son Gregory, 19, a violin student at Indiana University.

Dr. Walker grew up with music. His father, George Walker, was a physician who taught himself to play the piano and encouraged his son to devote his time to musical studies. His mother, Rosa King Walker, was a pianist who supervised his first lessons at age 5. His sister Frances became a concert pianist and is on the faculty of the Oberlin Conservatory of Music in Ohio.

"We had nothing but classical music growing up," recalled Dr. Walker, who earned his doctorate from the University of Rochester in 1957. "No one in the family had any interest in jazz. Most people find it hard to believe, but jazz was not an approved activity in most black cultural

mental soloists. symphony orchestras including the Baltimore Symphony ("Variations for Orchestra" and "Address for Orchestra") and chamber ensembles.

"Composition is a personal channel for me," he continued. "I'm not trying to use it as an emotional statement per se. But my writing has to be concerned about the effect it will have on a performer or an audience and have interest I strive for a different effect in different works."

Dr. Walker describes his life style—"The life of a teacher" with a full academic work load carefully interviews with critical concerts appearances and musical composition. The older son Gregory's 19-year-old violin student at Indiana University lives with him during the summer, and his younger son Ian, 11, will move this fall.

"I only travel to hear a performance when I am playing myself. I try to conserve my energy, because it's increasingly difficult to juggle three balls—practicing, composing and teaching," he said.

"I find teaching involves a part of my mind that needs to be involved. I am concerned how one can illuminate certain basic ideas to remove the kernel from the husk.

"It is important for me to know what standard I must reject. I must reject I find I reject quite a lot.

That sense of rejection carries over to his composing.

"My first consideration when I start thinking of a composition is, 'Is it something that has already been written or that I've heard on the street?' You have to know what to reject, which means you must know a lot of music.

"Then you shape what you want, which is in part what you know hasn't been done."

Then you sit down at the piano and begin writing.

circles, I know [Duke] Ellington came out of Washington, but jazz was relegated to night clubs.

Dr. Walker apparently was a precocious student, because after studying at Howard University's Junior Department, he graduated with honors as it from the Oberlin Conservatory of Music, then studied piano with Rudolf Serkin and Horszowski at Philadelphia's Curtis Institute and composition with Rosario Scalero.

In 1945 he made a "notable piano debut" in New York's Town Hall and played Rachmaninoff's 3d Piano Concerto with Eugene Ormandy and the Philadelphia Orchestra. His compositions have been played by leading vocal and instru-

This week's concerts at Cross Keys will be given by the Annapolis Brass Quintet at 12:30 p.m. Tuesday; the Piedmont Brass Quintet at 12:30 p.m. Thursday; and the Annapolis group at 7:30 p.m. Thursday and 12:30 p.m. Saturday.

my piano instructor at Oberlin. Bill had been a trombonist in the Boston Symphony before becoming the personnel manager of the orchestra.

Violin Sonata No. 2

The Kennedy Center for the Performing Arts in Washington, DC, commissioned me to compose a work for the violinist, Sanford Allen, who had been the only black instrumentalist in the New York Philharmonic for seventeen years. The Violin and Piano Sonata no. 2, a work in three movements, received its premiere in 1979 in the Terrace Theater of the Kennedy Center for the Performing Arts. The piano part in the first movement after the introduction represents an unusual concept. Its decorative staccato patterns create an accompaniment for the aspiring cantabile line in the solo violin part.

The second movement is a perpetual mobile that begins with irregular accented repeated notes. The third movement contains a quote from the spiritual "Let Us Break Bread Together." The pitches of the melody are distributed between the piano and violin parts. Also on the program in the Terrace Theater was a new violin and piano sonata by Roque Cordero.

1980s

Richard Kapp

Dick Kapp had met Eugene Fodor, a violinist who received a silver medal in the Tschaikowsky Competition in Moscow in 1974. Fodor's career had declined substantially and there were allegations about his use of drugs. His repertoire of showy concertos had made him vulnerable to criticism. Kapp advised Fodor to play contemporary music. Dick, with Fodor's approval, commissioned me to compose a violin concerto for him and the Philharmonia Virtuosi in 1983.

The first rehearsal of my concerto was scheduled to take place in 1984 in a church near Columbia University in New York. A snow storm enveloped the area the day before the rehearsal. It was impossible for some of the orchestra members to get to the church even after the rehearsal was pushed back a couple of hours.

Fodor, who had played a concert two days earlier in South America, arrived late. He was attired in cowboy boots and a Western-styled hat. A hacking cough made conversation difficult for him. But he managed to survive an inadequately prepared premiere with the Philharmonia Virtuosi at the state university in Poughkeepsie, New York. Paul Kapp, who had suffered a severe heart attack, bravely attended the performance using a cane to walk. This was the last time that I saw my great friend and benefactor.

Dick Kapp began to look for a buyer for General Music. EMI, with its eye on two lucrative songs, "I Left My Heart in San Francisco" and "The Singing Nun," purchased the entire catalog of General Music.

The main office of EMI was in California. It was staffed with persons from the pop world who identified symphonies as "songs." EMI had no interest in the considerable stock of contemporary American music that Paul Kapp had acquired. My efforts to recover possession of my music were successful after two years of attempting to find the right person who could understand my request. During that period EMI established two offices in New York City.

The entire catalog of General Music was discovered to have been placed in a warehouse in Pennsylvania. My scores were shipped to me in five large boxes. After having obtained my music, I began to look for another publisher. Although the New York Philharmonic had performed my *Overture: In Praise of Folly* and commissioned my Cello Concerto, efforts to solicit the interest of the underlings at G. Schirmer and Boosey and Hawkes were unproductive. The home offices of these companies are still disinclined to publish works by black classical composers. The current policy of Peters Music is no better in this respect.

MMB Music Publishers

I was introduced to the vice president of MMB Music, Douglas Jones, when he came to New York for a meeting. Like the brokers at EMI, he was only interested in my *Lyric for Strings*. We reached an agreement that resulted in my paying MMB Music two thousand dollars for the five boxes of my music that contained scores and parts, most of which had been engraved by Paul Kapp. MMB Music had begun to amass a large catalog of music by American composers in addition to handling music therapy publications and Orff educational materials.

MMB Music became my sole publisher after I was successful in retrieving scores from Associated Music Publishers and the Southern Publishing Co. Norman Goldberg, who founded MMB Music, passed the mantle of his presidency to his daughter, Marcia Goldberg. With over two hundred composers under her wing, it was not possible for her to adequately promote me even though I was said to be the most active of their composers. An online newsletter that was created was discontinued after less than a year. The family-owned company was sold to Lauren Keiser, formerly of Carl Fischer Music, in October of 2008. Under his leadership, there should be a significant expansion of the very limited investment that MMB Music had made for the distribution of my music.

Performances

When Zubin Mehta became the music director of the New York Philharmonic, Leon Thompson, director of educational activities, met with him to discuss the inclusion of music by black composers on the programs of the New York Philharmonic. A few weeks later, I received a telephone call from Leon, who wanted to know if I had an orchestral work that he could show to Mehta. I had nearly finished the orchestration of my second *Overture: In Praise of Folly*. (The first, written in my last year at Curtis with Scalero, had been trashed.) Thompson said that if I could bring it to the New York Philharmonic on the following Monday before noon, he would give it to Mehta. I had four days to finish the overture. Driving into New York an hour before the deadline, I found a parking space two blocks from Avery Fisher Hall. I dashed into the building and handed the score to Leon at 11:55 a.m. Three days later, Leon called to tell me that Mehta had decided to program the work.

The *Overture: In Praise of Folly* was performed seven times in 1981 by the New York Philharmonic. The sixth performance was in the Abyssinian Baptist Church in Harlem. It was Mehta's idea to take the orchestra uptown. Vans loaded with instruments clogged the entrance to the church on the narrow street on which the church is located. Inside the building the pulpit area bulged with string players. Enthusiasm for the program was infectious. The seventh performance was televised in Avery Fisher Hall for the Great Performances series of PBS. On the video of the performance of the *Overture*, Mehta can be heard saying as he walked off the stage, "Harlem was the best [performance]."

Robert Shaw, conductor of the Atlanta Symphony, programmed my *Address for Orchestra* for the opening concert of the season in September of 1981. Marcia Goldberg of MMB Music asked the administrators of the orchestra to invite me to attend that concert. This was the first complete performance of the work by a major American orchestra. James DePreist had performed the entire work in a festival in Mons, Belgium, in 1971. Robert Hughes had recorded the *Address* with the Oakland Youth Symphony for a Desto LP entitled *The Black Composer in America* in the 1970s. The third movement was taped in a concert by the Dallas Symphony for a documentary called *The Black Composer* produced by William Gaddis. The film was shown one time in 1972 during Black History Month by PBS. When I asked Channel 13 in New York about the possibility of airing the video again instead of the perennial Nat "King" Cole tape, Channel 13 admitted that the documentary that should have been in the Lincoln Center Library had been lost.

I was stricken by a recurrence of my ulcer and hospitalized in Mountainside Hospital in Montclair for a month just two days before the Atlanta performances. I received a telephone call from Robert Shaw while I was in a bed awaiting a serious operation. He said that he finally felt comfortable conducting contemporary music thirteen years after we met in Atlanta.

I received a tape of the first performance by the orchestra. Before playing the *Address*, Shaw delivered a poignant statement about my plight. He told me later that the second performance was the better of the two. But a cassette recording of the first performance remains the best that I have. Since I was unable to return to my teaching duties at Rutgers, I took a leave of absence for the second semester.

Several black composers were invited to attend performances of their works by both the Dallas and the Houston Symphony Orchestras. For the Dallas concert, Stephen Chambers, William Grant Still, and myself were hosted by a black couple who lived on the outskirts of the city in a well-kept brick ranch house with a swimming pool. Chambers, with whom I roomed, was going through his Sufi phase. He disappeared each night to emerge in time for the rehearsals. Still was a recluse. He may have been ill, since he made no effort to communicate with anyone.

David Baker was present for the Houston concert on which my *Spirituals* (now called *Folk Songs*) *for Orchestra* were played. I was not aware that he had a hairpiece until it flew off as we crossed the street after a rehearsal in the concert hall. The gusty wind pitched the wig in unpredictable spurts down the middle of the street until David ended its forward progress by stomping on it emphatically with his foot. I can imagine him thinking as his toe hit the pavement, "Enough of this."

Poem for Soprano and Chamber Ensemble

In the winter of 1982, while I was still recuperating at home from my operation, I began to work on one of my most provocative commissions. Capitol Chamber Artists in Albany, New York, had applied for and received a consortium grant from the National Endowment for the Arts (NEA). The other ensembles that had agreed to perform the new work were Collage in Boston and the New York New Music Ensemble. The latter group never played the work within a reasonable time as required by the NEA.

The *Poem* is a setting of the "Hollow Men" of T. S. Eliot for soprano and a chamber ensemble consisting of flute, clarinet, violin, cello, piano, harpsichord, guitar, and percussion. The guitar part was originally conceived for a harp. Mary Lou Saetta, the founder of Capitol Chamber Artists, said that she was not able to procure one. This seemed odd since some of the musicians that she engaged for her performances came from New York. Saetta had been a violinist in the Albany Symphony at one time. It's possible that the harpist in that orchestra did not want to work for her.

The T. S. Eliot poem is a scrambled collection of impressions. It is not an organic work. There is much that I like in Eliot's poetry—the rhythms and the outlandish allusions. But there are persons who have decried the racist statements attributed to this expatriate.

The poem conjures up associations of the underbelly of society, persons who are disconnected from the routine of daily living—the homeless. My score specifies that the soprano, second soprano, and the narrator should be clad in baggy, ill-fitting garments. The soprano walks out onto the stage carrying a sack of her possessions.

Before the music begins there is a preface, which I wrote and which is spoken by my younger son, Ian, on the Albany CD. The connection between the hallucinatory content of the text of the poem and the depressed condition of those persons who have lost their sense of purpose and direction can easily be made. There is something fundamentally disturbing to have a social statement ridiculed by critics who refuse to consider this relevancy, but who find nothing offensive to complain about in debased opera librettos and steamy ballet plots. Is the reality of this social condition inappropriately attached to this music? Does the reference to this condition activate an irrational disposition to have the music exist without any visual implications?

The soprano who sang the premiere of the *Poem* had note problems. Under her hat and scarf was rigged an electronic earpiece that transmitted pitches. After the premiere of the *Poem*, another singer, Janet Stasio, the wife of a local physician, was prepared for the recording of the work. Angelo Frascarelli, the conductor, shaped the production of every syllable of the text in private sessions with her. This was a dedicated effort on his part to have her project the intensity of the poem with the utmost clarity. Ms. Stasio's enunciation and her expressive delivery on the CD are beyond reproach.

Mary Lou Saetta was uncooperative when she was asked for her permission to use the recording of the *Poem*, originally made for Centaur Records, on my own Albany CD. Although I had helped her to make contact with Centaur Records and provided a friend's cover design for her CD, she remained adamant in rejecting my request. Centaur Records informed me that since she didn't own the tape master, they would give me permission to use the recording.

Cello Concerto

After the success of *In Praise of Folly*, Leon Thompson showed Albert "Nick" Webster, the managing director of the New York Philharmonic, the score of my *Dialogus for Cello and Orchestra*. Nick offered me a commission to compose a cello concerto for Lorne Munroe, the principal cellist of the New York Philharmonic. Nick voluntarily asked me to state my fee for the commission. The premiere in 1982 of the Cello Concerto was given in Avery Fisher Hall a year after the premiere of the *Overture: In Praise of Folly*. Zubin Mehta was again the conductor.

I was invited to attend a meeting in Avery Fisher Hall with Lorne Munroe and Zubin Mehta prior to the first rehearsal of my Cello

Concerto. Lorne played the solo cello part without accompaniment from beginning to end. Mehta made a few conducting gestures as I listened. Lorne had complete command of the difficulties in the score. There was no need to discuss anything with him.

The first rehearsal of the Cello Concerto was held in the Juilliard Theater because there was some renovation being done in Avery Fisher Hall. I was notified about a photo session that had been arranged before the beginning of the rehearsal. When I arrived at the theater, the photographer asked Mehta, Lorne Munroe, and me to pose in front of a Steinway D piano. The first page of the score of the concerto was opened. Mehta laughed as his finger pointed to the first measure and said "a-ha, four-four." (Since there are many meter changes in the work, I assumed that he was identifying the least problematic of them. He had little time to study the score, which was sent to him a few days before he left Vienna.)

Several days after the premiere I requested a copy of the photo taken at Juilliard. The photo made all three of us look a little silly. When the same picture had appeared with an article in the *New York Times* before the performances, the shot of Mehta had been excised.

There were only two performances of my Cello Concerto. The first performance on a very cold, damp evening was poorly attended. Empty seats were everywhere. Coughing was constant during the entire concert. In a review of the concert that appeared in the *New Yorker* magazine, Andrew Porter made the jingoistic asininity that I should have listened to the Elgar Cello Concerto before beginning my work. Donald Henahan of the *New York Times* also found the work incomprehensible.

When I applied for a Fromm Foundation grant to compose an orchestral work, I was awarded a small sum that did not include any copying costs. Gunther Schuller, who was the director of the foundation, told me that the basis for the disposition of the funds was the strong impression that the Cello Concerto had made on him.

I went backstage at the end of the first concert to thank Mehta for the performance. He was engaged in chewing out the associate principal in the violin section for missed entrances in the Mozart symphony that began the program. His ire also extended to another member of the orchestra who was not present. He wanted the orchestra manager to fire that person. I left the room without getting a chance to speak to him.

Mehta, nevertheless, had paid me a high compliment in describing the tutti in the Cello Concerto as "terrific." His willingness to program two of my orchestral works was in stark contrast to his predecessor, Leonard Bernstein, who never conducted any works by black composers. James Levine, Michael Tilson Thomas, and David Robertson are among other established American conductors who remain equally disinterested and oblivious of black composers' music.

I encountered George Perle, the composer, and his wife, Shirley, as I was leaving the backstage area. George was curious about the sound of the instrument that I used for the last chords in the orchestra to conclude the first movement of the concerto. I told him that it was a harpsichord. Shirley, who lived in Philadelphia when I was at Curtis, told me that Horszowski, who always seemed shy, had married for the first time at age ninety. I found that to be quite amusing. Then, I took the elevator to one of the rooms upstairs in Avery Fisher Hall where a few of my friends and Lorne's family were gathered for a buffet-styled dinner that Nick Webster had arranged.

Later in the year the Kennedy Center for the Performing Arts honored me with a concert in the Terrace Theater. The winner of the William Kapell International Piano Competition, Boris Slutsky, played a recital that included one of my works.

Bach Competition

The founder of the Bach International Competition, Raissa Tselentis, invited me to be a judge for this event. It was held in Georgetown University in Washington, DC. Ms. Tselentis had established this competition for pianists "out of gratitude" for being allowed to become an American citizen. Born in Greece, she had studied piano in Germany before emigrating to the United States. She and her husband lived in a tiny house in Georgetown, a small enclave on the western perimeter of the District of Columbia.

I was one of three judges. Gaby Casadesus, the widow of Robert Casadesus, and a German pedagogue were the other judges. All contestants were required to play the entire Goldberg Variations of Bach as their primary work in the preliminary round. A carpet led from the wings of the hall to the piano to insure that clacking heels would not reveal the women contestants. The judges were hidden behind a screen that eliminated the possibility of identifying the pianists.

We listened for two days before the process of elimination began. Secret ballots did not produce a unanimous decision. My tallies were virtually identical to those of the German judge. Mme. Casadesus's tabulation was awry.

Ms. Tselentis arranged for us to have dinner at the home of the French cultural attaché in Washington, DC. The four-course meal with roast duck as the entree was fabulous. Each judge was asked to make a few succinct remarks. As I had already imbibed two glasses of red wine (one is normally my limit), my comments after the champagne probably reduced my toast to gibberish. I couldn't recall what I said.

The next day we were driven to the White House where we met Rosalind Carter. Later, there was a ceremony on the lawn. Lady Bird Johnson, widow of President Lyndon Johnson, sat two rows in front of us. President Jimmy Carter awarded a medal to a retired admiral who had been one of his instructors at the naval academy. The competition winner played Bach for the occasion.

Ms. Tselentis was a passionate advocate of the music of Bach. She was a great admirer of my piano music. After a long illness she died at age eighty-six.

American Academy

In 1982 I received an award from the American Academy of Arts and Letters. I arrived early at 633 West 155th Street in New York before most persons had gathered for the reception that preceded the luncheon. I was seated at a table in a large room when I was approached by the director of the Yaddo Colony, Curtis Harnack. He had brought along a freshly cleaned necktie that I had left in my cabin several years earlier. An uncomfortable hernia had caused me to shorten my residency in Saratoga Springs, New York. Combating the flies and mosquitos in my cabin added to the misery of my condition.

At the reception at the academy, I spoke briefly with Ulysses Kay, the only black composer who was a member of this august organization. Toni Morrison congratulated me and then disappeared quickly before I could converse with her. At the end of the ceremonies, Ralph Ellison invited me to his apartment. Greeting me warmly when I arrived after finally finding a parking space several blocks away, he went to a bookcase, picked up a cassette tape, and waved it in the air. He said, "You see, I taped your concert (with the Philharmonic)." He was referring to

American Academy of Arts and Letters members' dinner, January 19, 2000. Front row, left to right: George Walker, Andrew Imbrie, Robert Ward, George Perle, and Yehudi Wyner. Back row, left to right: Lukas Foss, Ned Rorem, Jack Beeson, and Gunther Schuller

the PBS televised program on which *In Praise of Folly* was heard. We had an enjoyable conversation as he sipped a few drinks.

Several years later I called his home to arrange a meeting for my son, Ian, with him. At that time Ian had written two novels before deciding to concentrate on playwriting. Ellison's wife told me that he was working. I was not aware that he was already ill. Unfortunately, he was not able to finish *Junteenth*, his second novel. There are many extraordinary passages in the collected and edited sketches published as a narrative that accurately and poetically recall the ambiance of the pre–civil rights era.

Cantata

I was approached by Walter Turnbull, director of the Boys Choir of Harlem, who was interested in commissioning a work for his choir and a chamber orchestra. I accepted a meager fee to write the score. The premiere of my Cantata was given in Alice Tully Hall in New York in June of 1982. The work utilizes a tenor and a soprano soloist. It is in two movements consisting of a setting of the Twenty-third Psalm and a portion of the Twenty-fourth Psalm in the King James Version of the Bible. Recordings of it were made in Japan and in this country by the Boys Choir of Harlem. The slightly harsh tonal quality of the choir was mitigated in the American recording by the warm acoustic of St. George's Episcopal Church in lower Manhattan, where Harry T. Burleigh had been a soloist. Greater attention was given to rhythm by Turnbull.

At the first rehearsal of the Cantata that I attended, the boys stood at attention for the entire time, about fifty minutes, in an autocratic demonstration that I found excruciating to watch. I finally asked Turnbull to let them be seated. He was the tenor soloist in the concert and on the recordings. The soprano, Joyce Mathis, was a fine collaborator. The mission of the Boys Choir of Harlem was undermined by Turnbull's refusal to comply with a court-ordered mandate and a burdensome accumulated debt.

Eastman Tour

The Eastman School of Music planned a tour of four cities for the Eastman Philharmonia, the student orchestra. I was commissioned to compose a work with the proscribed title, *An Eastman Overture*. Incorporated in the score are quotes from the three Bs—Bach, Beethoven, and Brahms. Bach was represented by an excerpt from the great organ fugue from the Fantasia and Fugue in A Minor. A fragment from the first movement of the Beethoven String Quartet, op. 135, appears in augmentation and a snippet from the Brahms Intermezzo in B-flat Minor, op. 117—which I played on my debut recital at Howard University in 1937—is also imbedded in the score.

The orchestra began the tour with a concert in the Kennedy Center in Washington, DC, in 1983. The program was comprised entirely of American music. The next concerts were in the Academy of Music in Philadelphia, Carnegie Hall, and Heinz Hall in Pittsburgh. The final concert was in the Eastman Theatre. The acoustics of Carnegie Hall (before its renovation) were clearly the best of all of the auditoriums.

When I first met the conductor of the Eastman Philharmonia, David Effron, he told me that he was perplexed by my score. The performances became better when they were repeated. Part of the concert program was recorded by Polygram Records. The cover of the LP sported a photo of Willie Stargell, a former first baseman of the Pittsburgh Pirates, wearing a Pirate cap on his head. (Robert Freeman, the director of the Eastman School at that time, was a baseball fanatic.) The photo of an athlete on the cover of a serious musical production was not the best example of good taste and judgment.

Stargell narrated the text of Schwantner's "New Morning for the World" rather self-consciously despite having had considerable coaching. The recitation of the final quotes from Dr. Martin Luther King's speeches is supported by Hansonesque harmonies that sound dated. No liner notes were included in the jacket. Most surprising to me was the decision by Eastman to release the recording in only two formats, an LP and a cassette, but not as a CD.

Piano Sonata No. 4

A link to my former piano teacher, David Moyer, was established when I received a telephone call from Betsy Moyer, his daughter-in-law, in 1983. Her son, Frederick Moyer, a fine pianist, had played concerts in many countries. Betsy told me that the Pew Charitable Fund in Philadelphia would fund a commission for Fred if I wrote a solo piano work for him. He would give the premiere of it in New York.

When I finished the score of my Sonata no. 4 for Piano, Fred and I spent several hours working out every detail of the work in my home and discussing it in several telephone conversations. In the second of the two movements there is a quote from the spiritual "Sometimes I Feel like a Motherless Child." After giving the New York premiere in Merkin Hall, Fred recorded the sonata for GM Records.

1990s

Poeme for Violin and Orchestra

The rough performance of my Violin Concerto by the Philharmonia Virtuosi of New York prompted me to make some revisions of the score, although I knew that the orchestra was at fault for some of the problems. There is an underlying unrest in the concerto-lyrical moments in the solo violin part and more turbulent ones in the orchestra. The second movement begins with a forceful timpani solo. The final section of the third movement is free of the angst that precedes it. The transformation reflects the resignation and acceptance of the passing of my mother. The work is dedicated to her.

The title was changed to *Poeme for Violin and Orchestra* to suggest the melodious qualities of the music. I contacted Cho-Liang Lin, a violinist whose recordings I had heard. He spoke to Hugh Wolff, the conductor of the New Jersey Symphony and the Saint Paul Chamber Orchestra, about the *Poeme*. Wolff agreed to program the work. Lin played it three times in Saint Paul and three times with the New Jersey Symphony in 1991. The seventh performance was given by the New Jersey Symphony in Carnegie Hall. In a review of the first performance in Saint Paul the *Poeme* was called the best new work of that season.

Orpheus

Edwin London had left Smith College in 1968, the same year that I became a visiting professor at the University of Colorado. After going to the University of Illinois, Ed founded a chamber orchestra at Cleveland State University that focused on presenting concerts of contemporary American music. When I received a commission from the Cleveland

Chamber Symphony, I chose the myth of Orpheus for a work that employs a narrator.

Episodes are announced by a speaker as the myth unfolds. The narrator assumes several roles. By changing the quality and tone of his voice, he represents Orpheus, Pluto, and the father of Orpheus, Oeagrus.

The wedding of Orpheus and Eurydice suggested the incorporation of a dance episode. This idea presented itself after I recalled a segment in the film *Zorba the Greek*. In a scene on a beach, Anthony Quinn is asked by his "boss" to teach him to dance. But I did not attempt to give this section of the score an ethnic quality.

The music begins with an oboe solo accompanied by pizzicato octaves in the strings in an irregular pulse. It becomes more frenetic, accelerating into a fugato. The termination of this section presages the tragedy that follows—the death of Eurydice. Orpheus encounters Pluto in the underworld. After Orpheus receives permission to leave the underworld with his wife, he violates the instruction given to him by Pluto. In looking back he causes Eurydice to vanish "to become a shade." Eurydice is briefly represented by a woman's voice as she cries out for Orpheus upon her return to the underworld.

The introductory chords played on a harp at the beginning of *Orpheus* and at its end suggest the use of a lyre. The narrative that I wrote underscores the relationship between father and son in the beginning of the work and at its end in addition to the mythic portrayal of Orpheus and Eurydice. A four-note motive derived from the syllables of Eurydice (two short and two long accents in the Latin pronunciation) is used in the orchestra and spoken by members of the orchestra as Orpheus searches for his bride. It has a pathetic and distressed quality. The narrator's agonized voice in the final section laments, "My son, my son." In this version Orpheus is torn to bits by Thracian women. A single harp note, a tear, is repeated to bring closure to this tragedy "as it as been preserved and imparted to us." The premiere of *Orpheus* was in 1994.

Organ Commissions

The Washington, DC, chapter of the American Guild of Organists commissioned *Prayer* and *Improvisation on St. Theodulph* for an organ recital in 1997. "All Glory, Laud, and Honor" was one of my father's favorite hymn tunes. The following year I received a commission to compose a work for the National Convention of the American Guild of Organists that was held in Denver, Colorado, in 1998.

I was told that there had never been a black organist to present a concert at these conventions. I stipulated in the contract that was drawn up that the commissioned work would be performed on a program selected by a black organist. In the sweaty confines of a modern church outside of Denver, where the temperature inside hovered around ninety-five degrees, Mickey Thomas Terry gave the premiere of *Spires* for organ. The simulation of feathered creatures in the bell tower can be imagined in one section of the work. The final two chords are played fortissimo only on a coupled manual, without the use of the pedals, to create a freely resonant sound in the upper reaches of a sanctuary.

Discrimination Case

Rutgers University, in violation of a national law against age discrimination, instituted an age ceiling for tenured faculty. Professors were forced to retire when they became seventy years old, my age in 1992. This was mandatory. No exceptions were allowed. The administrators in the university had connived with the state legislature to save quite a bit of money by resorting to this illegal policy for several years. Full professors with years of teaching experience became expendable. The quality of instruction was considerably diminished. Money saved may have been channeled to the Rutgers athletic department to increase efforts to attain national prominence for its football team.

With retirement inevitable, I decided to protest a decision made by the dean and provost that had affected my income for three years. The chairman of the Music Department, Kenneth Wilson, had given me the highest recommendation for a merit award. The provost, Norman Samuels, gave the award each year to Lewis Porter, a jazz pianist, whose rating was well below mine, after the dean of the college, David Hosford, had eliminated my name from consideration.

I discussed the misappropriation with the campus representative of the AAUP (American Association of University Professors). A meeting was arranged with Samuels, who staunchly defended the character of Hosford, a close friend of his. Samuels, however, could not justify the dean's choice of a jazz pianist. An article about the discrimination appeared in the *Star-Ledger*, the principal newspaper in New Jersey.

The university agreed to pay me five thousand dollars while denying any wrongdoing.

Before the agreement was reached, Samuels demeaned my contribution to the Music Department. For years before this incident he had voiced the opposite opinion. I was a "jewel" in the ranks of the university's professors. With the collapse of Rutgers' music education program in 1992, the Music Department ceased to exist as a separate entity. Course requirements for a major in music became pathetically limited.

Albany Records

I was invited by my publisher, MMB Music, to attend some of the sessions of the American Symphony Orchestra League in New York City in 1992. This is an event that takes place in different cities each year. I was introduced to Peter Kermani, president of Albany Records, as I was leaving a presentation. When I told him that I wanted to make recordings of some of my music, he suggested that I send him the edited masters when they were finished. This was an unusual offer.

My first CD, *George Walker in Recital* was released in 1994. Other releases from Albany Records, *George Walker: A Portrait* and *George Walker*, contain works that had been recorded previously on LPs. I was able to secure the master tapes of my Cello Sonata, Antiphonys, *Music for Brass (Sacred and Profane)*, and the Variations for Orchestra that had been placed in the *Rodgers and Hammerstein Archives for Recorded Sound* by Dick Kapp. They were transferred to the CD format.

On the *George Walker* CD, the violinist heard in my Violin and Piano Sonata no. 1 is my son Gregory. We recorded the sonata in my home. The first CD launched a highly compatible relationship with Susan Bush and Peter Kermani of Albany Records that allows me to choose my own repertoire for production under their aegis. My most recent CDs made for this label are *George Walker: Great American Orchestral Works, Vol. 1* and *George Walker: Great American Chamber Works*.

Recording

My interest in tape recording began in 1960. I had met Fritz Steinhardt, who was a professor of mathematics at City College of New York, through Esther Aronauskaite when I was at Curtis. Fritz could hardly wait to finish his classes before returning to his apartment at 315 River-side Drive. He used a timer to record Mozart concertos from radio station WQXR on his Tandberg 5 tape recorder. Fritz and his first wife created Lea Pocket scores, miniaturized Xeroxed copies of Urtext editions of Bach, painstakingly pasted together. These were sold to Kalmus Editions. Fritz invited me for lunch on one occasion. We were joined by a friend of his, who was Albert Einstein's assistant at Princeton.

I had purchased a Zenith portable radio shortly after I left Dillard University in 1955. When I bought a Uher Tape Recorder, I was not able to properly connect the two units in order to record FM broadcasts. The saga of numerous stereo systems began with the acquisition of a Sherwood Stereo Receiver and a Tandberg 7 tape recorder. This was a beautiful unit in a wooden case. But with audible wow and flutter, it was not a professional recorder.

Fritz had amassed a large collection of four-track tapes. Without careful documentation it was difficult to locate musical material that had been recorded this way to economize on tape. Choosing an Ampex 350 tape recorder, a two-track machine, was the first step that I took to obtain the best reproduction. But taping FM broadcasts on two tracks was more expensive than recording on a four-track Tandberg. I used the Ampex 350 primarily to record my piano playing. My observations about piano recording were published in an article entitled "Piano Sound in Reproduction" in the *Music Journal* in 1964.

After becoming a professor emeritus from Rutgers University, I purchased a Nagra-D (digital tape) recorder. My previous tape recorders were analog units. When I was teaching at Smith College, I had mentioned to Alvin Etler, who was the composition teacher in the Music Department, that I wanted to make commercial recordings of some of the piano repertoire that I had played in concerts. Alvin remarked that the most difficult aspect of this quest would be in finding a conduit for the distribution of the recordings. With the encouragement that I received from the president of Albany Records, Peter Kermani, this concern became nonexistent.

There were certain significant advantages that the Nagra-D recorder offered. It was portable. It could record two tracks for two hours at a sampling rate of 44.1 or one hour at 96.2. With a tape counter, it was easy to locate takes that were made. I could operate the machine without additional help when I recorded my piano playing. This Swiss-made unit was capable of producing the finest quality of sound available and the most accurate from any source. John Taylor, the manufacturer of a fine ribbon speaker called the Yankee, told me that he used my first CD to tune his speakers.

Lilacs for Voice and Orchestra

The Boston Symphony requested some of my scores from MMB Music in 1995. I had no reason to expect that I would receive a letter from this organization informing me that I had been chosen for a commission relating to a special event. I had submitted numerous scores to this orchestra in the past without any acknowledgment of their receipt or without any interest expressed in them.

The commission was for a work for tenor and orchestra, eight minutes in duration. It would be performed on concerts honoring the celebrated black tenor Roland Hayes in February of 1996.

The selection of a text for the commission was as time-consuming as the composition of the work. After perusing numerous anthologies in my library and that of the Montclair Public Library, I chose the poem "When Lilacs Last in the Dooryard Bloom'd" by Walt Whitman. The poem was written in 1865 after the assassination of President Abraham Lincoln. It is an elegy that contains three recurring symbols—the lilac, a star, and a bird.

Since the commission was for a short work, I decided to use only four of the thirteen stanzas—the first, second, third, and the thirteenth. These comprise the four movements of *Lilacs*. The opening motive stated by the horn reappears at the beginning of the fourth movement. The third movement recalls my first visit with my family to our cousin Lila's home in Northumberland County, Virginia. The vague recollection of her plot of land underscores the text "In the dooryard fronting an old farmhouse . . ." Stronger still in my memory were the delicious hot buttered biscuits, corn pudding, and fried chicken that she served that surpassed any similar dishes that I have experienced. Waiting several hours beyond our normal mealtime for breakfast and dinner was painful, but ultimately rewarding.

In the fourth movement, after an orchestral introduction that suggests the chatter of birds, the first notes for the singer are the pitches from the spiritual "Li'l Boy How Old Are You?" which was made famous by Roland Hayes. The answer in the song is "Sir, I'm only twelve years old." This was approximately my age when my piano teacher introduced me to Roland Hayes at Howard University.

The use of motives for the lilac and the bird in a single text creates a formal unity that is not found in the *Four Last Songs of Strauss*. Textures stemming from the use of a large orchestra in *Lilacs* are more colorful than those in Barber's *Knoxville Summer of 1915* and the climaxes are more vivid. By contrast, the orchestral setting of the entire Whitman poem by Paul Hindemith, who was commissioned by Robert Shaw, has a Germanic quality to it. Like the score of Roger Sessions, it employs a chorus. *Lilacs* is an atonal work.

The parades in which my high school cadet corps participated on national holidays followed the same route down Pennsylvania Avenue in Washington, DC, that Lincoln's funeral procession had taken. As a native Washingtonian I had a certain visual advantage over the other composers who had set this poetry to music.

I completed *Lilacs* in six weeks. It was twice the length specified in the contract. When I told the artistic administrator, Tony Fogg, that it was finished, he asked me to come to Tanglewood in August of 1995 to show the score to Seiji Ozawa, the conductor of the Boston Symphony. When we met in the Koussevitzky House, I played the entire work—solo tenor and orchestral parts—from the piano score.

Ozawa, scrunched over the piano, emitted occasional grunts in solfege as he scanned the orchestral score. Vinson Cole, the tenor whom Ozawa had chosen for the solo part, and Fogg, the artistic administrator, were also present. They followed the piano score in the audition. When I finished playing, Cole had a puzzled expression on his face. Ozawa pointed to a passage in the orchestral score that he said was unplayable. I was dumbfounded. Surely, I thought, the violins of the great Boston Symphony could play those notes. And they did, without any changes being made.

Before I had completed the score of the commissioned work, Fogg called me to ask what the title of it would be. I told him that I was considering several titles, one of which was *Melisma*. The potential title referred to the embellished vocal part. When the publicity for the 1995–1996 concert season was announced in the fall, I was surprised that he had unilaterally chosen that title. After I finished the score, I called the work, *Lilacs for Tenor and Orchestra*.

In November, Fogg told me that the tenor, Vinson Cole, had gone to Australia with his coach for some concerts. When Cole returned to

World Premiere of Lilacs, February 1, 1996, with soprano Faye Robinson, conductor Seiji Ozawa, and the Boston Symphony

the United States, he admitted that he couldn't sing the solo part in *Lilacs*. Fogg was desperate. When he asked me if I would agree to having a soprano sing the tenor part, I told him that this was an acceptable alternative. He engaged Faye Robinson, who had sung works of Michael Tippett with the Boston Symphony.

She called me to discuss the range of the solo part. I would not allow her to change a note that was used in the previous measure. But because the lower part of her range was weak, I agreed to have her sing a few notes an octave higher than they were written. The title of the work was changed again to *Lilacs for Voice and Orchestra*.

The concerts by the Boston Symphony were part of a citywide celebration of Roland Hayes. There were lectures in museums on his life, a video was shown continuously in Symphony Hall, free CDs of his *My Favorite Spirituals* were distributed to schoolchildren, and a pre-concert dinner was arranged for invited guests.

Several of Hayes's former pupils came to Boston for the premiere of *Lilacs*. One of these singers was John Hornor III, a bass-baritone from New York and the father-in-law of Yo-Yo Ma, the cellist. The mayor of Boston was present. AT&T was the sponsor for this memorial event. There were four performances of the program in February of 1996. A glowing review appeared in the *Boston Globe*. (Months later I learned that Lloyd Schwarz of the *Boston Phoenix* newspaper wrote a disparaging review of Faye Robinson's singing and the entire concert. He may have been stewed at the time, since everything hurt his tender ears.)

The authenticity of the performance of *Lilacs* by the Boston Symphony was affected by a compromise. Three measures before the end of the work a celesta in the orchestral score is required to be played simultaneously with a harpsichord. The management of the Boston Symphony refused to pay for an additional player for that part. Union regulations forbade another orchestra member to play it.

Several years after the premiere of *Lilacs*, the Boston Symphony issued twelve CDs of broadcast performances. The Roland Hayes tribute was not included in this series. A similar omission was made in an archival release by the New York Philharmonic. My Cello Concerto that was commissioned by this orchestra was excluded. An arrangement for orchestra of Ellington's Harlem was the token work from a black composer.

Winning the Pulitzer

PULITZER PRIZE

$\mathcal{I}$ was able to obtain a tape of the premiere performance of *Lilacs*. In talking with the recording engineer for the Boston Symphony after a rehearsal, I impressed her with my knowledge of the B&K Microphones that were suspended in Symphony Hall. These were her favorite mikes. She facilitated the release of a cassette tape. It was submitted with the score to the Pulitzer Prize jury just before the entry deadline, March 1, 1996.

The announcement about my receiving the Pulitzer Prize in Music came from a telephone call from Frances Richard, director of concert music at ASCAP (American Society of Composers, Authors and Publishers). She had been told that information about the Pulitzer Prize awards would be released at 3:00 p.m. that day. I had been proofreading at my piano the engraved copy of an organ work, *Prayer*. It was composed exactly fifty years after my *Lyric for Strings*. The phone had rung a couple of times before Fran called. I was reluctant to pick up the receiver again. When she told me the news, I could only shout "Wow" a couple of times.

The Pulitzer Prizes are awarded in an unostentatious ceremony at Columbia University. A reception during which delicious barbecued shrimp were passed around by student waiters preceded a mediocre luncheon. The entree was a bland portion of white fish. Five or six persons were seated at a table in a rather large room. One guest was allowed for each recipient of a prize. There were approximately eight to ten tables.

Section 4 | The Sunday Star-Ledger **Spotlight** April 14, 1996

MUSIC

Music community says Pulitzer long overdue

BY MICHAEL REDMOND

From Boston to Berlin, they're all saying the same thing. The award of the Pulitzer Prize in music to George Walker, a long-time resident of Montclair, is recognition long overdue.

There's a resonance in the choice to honor any individual that inevitably travels outward toward the broader community. It so happens that George Walker, 73, is the first black American composer to receive one of his native land's highest musical honors. The message — this is not to say it was conscientiously intended — is simple. The level of musical distinction appropriate for blacks is not limited to jazz, pop, rock, rap or any other distant relation of the minstrel show.

"This composer has finally gotten the recognition he deserves. I hope this prize convinces colleagues of mine around the United States to play his music. That's the important thing, to play the music," said Zubin Mehta, who has conducted five of Walker's orchestra pieces with the New York Philharmonic.

Speaking from Berlin, the world-famous maestro characterized Walker's music as "out of the ordinary" for its "innovative fusion of two elements — the highest level of classical craftsmanship and a profound respect, indeed love, for the historical folk tradition" of black American music.

In Monte Carlo, American conductor James DePreist also applauded Tuesday's news that "Lilacs," a 16-minute work for solo voice and orchestra premiered in February by the Boston Symphony Orchestra, had won the prize for Walker.

"There are composers whose works you encounter and admire, who have distinguished reputations and who go to their graves without receiving this kind of recognition. Winning the Pulitzer is a defining moment," said DePreist, who brought Walker's Address for Orchestra (1959) to European audiences.

"The fact that George is the first black to win is a commentary. Are we bragging or complaining? Clearly this composer deserves the honor because of the quality of his work. His race isn't

HONORED COMPANY — Pulitzer Prize-winning composer George Walker (far right) with Boston Symphony conductor Seiji Ozawa and tenor Vinson Cole (center).

relevant. The consideration is artistic — you consider the work, period." the conductor said.

That's right, of course, but questions linger. William Grant Still (1895-1978), composer of Afro-American Symphony (1930) and much other lasting music, never won. Ulysses Kay (1917-1995), another important black composer, never won. The black American who many would describe as one of the most important figures in the history of American music — Duke Ellington — never won.

In 1965 the Pulitzer music committee privately voted to award Ellington a "special prize" for "the vitality and originality of his total production." The committee was overruled because Ellington was, you know, a mere jazz musician.

When informed of this decision, Ellington, then 66 years old, said that "fate is being kind to me. Fate doesn't want me to be famous too young."

DePreist recalled the quandary black Americans faced when his aunt, the late Marian Anderson, made her Metropolitan Opera debut in 1955. Anderson was the first black singer to star there. The recognition came very late in her illustrious career.

"When my aunt finally sang at the Met, it seemed there were only two actions — there was elation, and there was the concomitant question why it had taken the Met so long to ask her.

My aunt's response was to celebrate. Her attitude was, once an honor is given for the right reason, it's natural and correct to celebrate."

Clement Alexander Price of Newark, a nationally distinguished historian of the black American experience, interpreted Walker's Pulitzer as signifying "outstanding achievement by an American composer whose distinction is known by far too few of his countrymen, even by some longtime academic colleagues. George labored for years in the vineyards of Rutgers, teaching, composing, without enough people realizing what quality of man they had here."

Sad to say, Rutgers University wins the booby prize in the George Walker story. The composer, who confined his remarks to saying that "the university treated me very badly" at the close of his 23-year tenure in Newark, remains bitter that he was repeatedly passed over for merit awards. In 1992 he accused David Hosford, dean of the Newark campus, of racial discrimination. The dispute was settled privately.

The bias flap astonished people who knew Walker, an intensely private man who is not the sort of person to play the race card lightly. The composer has long been adamant in his insistence that standard of achievement is the point, not the race of those struggling to achieve.

"There is no equal opportunity" in art, Walker has flatly said — talent, discipline and drive are not equally distributed among people, no matter their race. Walker has criticized "the potpourri of jazz, gospel and classical music contrived as 'special' concerts by some orchestras, which offer this as a token for predominantly black audiences."

He has also insisted that "we have to recognize that classical music is elitist by nature. It is more demanding of the listener, and its rewards will not appeal to many persons. And so the black composer is already ensconced in a niche that has limited exposure."

Walker's rigorous standard has appealed to some of America's finest orchestras, including the New York Philharmonic and the Cleveland Orchestra, as well as the Royal Philharmonic (London) and the John F. Kennedy Center for the Performing Arts in Washington, which commissions music. The number of works by Walker that have been commercially recorded is about par with those by Milton Babbitt, George Crumb and Elliott Carter, also contemporary American composers of international repute.

Walker — who composes "all over the house," he says, and not just in the living area dominated by LPs, CDs, six-foot mahogany speakers and a grand piano — is currently working on some pieces for pipe organ commissioned by the American Guild of Organists.

Robert Pollock, artistic director of the Composers Guild of New Jersey and a composer himself, said that Walker is "a perfectionist who once told me that he works very slowly, sometimes as slowly as one or two notes a day. His compositions are usually not long, but they exhibit an intense condensation of inspiration. A listener can feel that every note in a Walker score is there because it has been listened to and thought about for a long time."

Another facet of Walker's artistry is his "amazing" pianistic gifts, Pollock said.

"When the Composers Guild presented George Walker in recital in the Noyes Museum, his playing, his interpretation, they were absolutely stunning. Walker is quiet and reserved — I would say he is a shy man. So I just wasn't expecting the kind of playing I heard."

Star-Ledger article, April 14, 1996

The president of Columbia University, George Rupp, sat next to me on my right. My son Ian was on my left. Across from us was Rick Bragg of the *New York Times.* (After being accused in 2003 of using the reports of a freelance journalist for an article, he resigned from the *New York Times.*) There was a very brief speech by Rupp after the entree,

With my son Ian at the Pulitzer ceremony

tasteless vanilla ice cream for dessert, and a few words from Sissela Bok representing the Pulitzer Prize board. President Rupp handed out from a small platform a Tiffany crystal paperweight and a certificate in a light blue, leather-padded diploma case (Columbia University's color) to each recipient of the prize after his name and the designation of the award was announced. When the last prizewinner left the platform, the ceremony was officially over.

After I received the phone call from Fran Richard, reporters began to line up outside of my front door within the hour. There wasn't a parking space available on the street for several blocks. The men politely took turns in entering my house. The first reporter to appear was Ralph Blumenthal of the *New York Times*. The fine article that he wrote was quite accurate with one exception: my younger son, Ian, submitted the application for the Pulitzer Prize, not my older son, Gregory.

When Blumenthal asked me about the problem that I had with Rutgers University over merit awards, I declined to go into the details of my confrontation with Norman Samuels, the provost of Rutgers University in Newark. Syndicated press agencies gave the announcement of the prize extraordinary coverage in the United States and in Europe. But the Boston Symphony has not performed *Lilacs* since its premiere.

In 1997 I received honorary doctorates from Montclair State University, Bloomfield College, and the Curtis Institute of Music. My first honorary doctorate from Lafayette College in 1982 was unexpected, since I had only a tangential connection with the college. I had played a piano recital there on very short notice after confusing the date of the program. The other recipients of honorary degrees from Lafayette College were Senator Bill Bradley of basketball fame, a Democratic candidate for president, and Dick Thornburgh, governor of Pennsylvania. The next year, 1983, I received a doctor of music degree from Oberlin College. Another degree with the same title was conferred on me by Spelman College in 2001.

Winning the Pulitzer Prize did not result in an avalanche of commissions. There was an unusual request from Frances Steiner, the conductor of a community orchestra, who wanted to give the West Coast premiere of *Lilacs*. She conjoined this orchestra with a student orchestra to give a performance in which the challenges in the music were met and overcome with relief and great exhilaration.

When Lyn McLain, founder and conductor of the DC Youth Orchestra, phoned to tell me that he wanted to present a program in my honor, he was flabbergasted to learn that no one in Washington, DC, had congratulated me on having received the Pulitzer Prize in Music. My association with the DC Youth Orchestra began in the 1970s when my *Address for Orchestra* was played in Europe on the first tour of the orchestra. It was performed in a competition for youth orchestras.

An elegant ceremony was arranged in June of 1997 as part of a donation drive. A table could be purchased for $250. A black-tie reception was followed by a fine dinner in a building close to the National Gallery of Art. An honor guard of young men and women from the cadet program at Dunbar High School marched into the room and presented arms before I received a citation and was asked to speak to the guests. The DC Youth Orchestra played *Folk Songs*. It was conducted by Michael Morgan to end the event. Mayor Marion Barry designated June 17 as George Walker Day in Washington, DC, and I received a citation from President Bill Clinton.

I met Joseph McClellan, the music critic for the *Washington Post*, after leaving the booth of an FM station in Washington, DC, where I had an interview before the DC Youth Orchestra ceremony. He said that he always wanted to write an article about me. We met later in the

FM station to discuss my career. In the article that was published in the *Washington Post*, I was called the finest classical composer born in Washington, DC.

No major orchestra in the country attempted to contact me about performing the Pulitzer Prize work or any other orchestral work of mine. This lack of interest highlights the schism that exists between the significance of this preeminent award and an appropriate acknowledgment of it by the artistic administrators, marketing personnel of major orchestras, and conductors.

Richard Wernick, who was the chairman of the Pulitzer Prize jury that gave me the award, was most cordial when he called to congratulate me. He told me that I could expect to be asked to be on the jury for the selection of future awardees. Thirteen years have passed since I received the prize. I have not been invited to participate in the adjudication. The year after Melinda Wagner was chosen for the prize, she became a member of the jury.

A year after I received the Pulitzer Prize, my friend, Ed London, conducted three of my works on a program at Cleveland State University in 1997. My son Gregory was the soloist in a splendid performance of my *Poeme for Violin and Orchestra* that was unfairly denigrated by Donald Rosenberg. (Rosenberg was recently demoted from his position as the chief critic of the *Cleveland Plain Dealer* because of his consistently obstreperous reviews.) The other two works on the program were *Orpheus* and the *Lyric for Strings*. After that concert, these works and *Folk Songs for Orchestra* were recorded for Albany Records. A grant from the National Endowment for the Arts was the funding source. *Folk Songs* had been premiered in a revised version by David Zinman and the Baltimore Symphony in 1992.

· 6 ·

Further Successes

RECORDING COMPANIES

$\mathcal{W}$ith the expectation that there would be some interest in recording *Lilacs for Voice and Orchestra*, I contacted several record companies. Andrew Cornall of Decca Records in London was clearly disingenuous. Deutsche Grammophon's vague response reflected a lack of interest in contemporary music.

When I contacted Sony Classical, my initial conversation with Steven Paul, one of their top administrators, was encouraging. He shuttled back and forth every month from Hamburg, Germany, to New York. After having had lunch with him in his office on two occasions, he told me that he would propose a recording contract for me when he returned in two weeks from Hamburg. When he arrived in New York, he found that he had been subverted and his office appropriated. Peter Gelb had been installed as the czar of Sony Classical.

Gelb had hired a young assistant, Rosemary Holland, who had recently come to New York from England. When I made an appointment with her, she seemed to be sincerely convinced that the tapes that she heard merited consideration. Despite my desire to have my orchestral music played for Gelb, she insisted that he should hear my songs first. Her inexperience and naïveté did not prepare her for the machinations of the corporate world. Gelb informed her that there was no market for these works. He had just contracted a black gospel singer.

IMPACT OF THE *LYRIC FOR STRINGS*

The *Lyric for Strings* has always received highly complimentary reviews since its first public performance in Washington, DC. What is particularly curious is that no one at Curtis, student or faculty, has ever made a comment about it—not after the radio performance, not after the student performance of the entire String Quartet no. 1 in Casimir Hall, nor when Gian-Carlo Menotti was present for a reading of it in one of his classes. Boulanger had listened to a string quartet's performance of it at Fontainebleau in 1958 without saying anything. But she habitually avoided making comments about any performance.

The quality of performances of the *Lyric for Strings* varies from the very mediocre to the exceptional. Many persons and even some conductors dearly love the work. Obtaining a good performance of it is not easy. I asked Paul Freeman to record it with an orchestra in Mexico. He sent me two cassettes and a digital audiotape of what he had done. All were bad and unusable. His most recent recording on Cedille is also bad. But other conductors have also produced mediocre results. Riccardo Muti conducted *Lyric for Strings* with the Philadelphia Orchestra in a Martin Luther King concert. The jerky playing and the unsynchronized pizzicati from a major orchestra were embarrassing.

When Andrew Davis conducted the Chicago Symphony in two of the four performances of the *Lyric for Strings* that I attended, I received a standing ovation each time for the six-and-a-half-minute work. He had conducted it ten years earlier in a joint concert involving the New York Philharmonic and an all-state orchestra in Avery Fisher Hall in New York.

Hugh Wolff's performances of it with the New Jersey Symphony and the Saint Paul Chamber Orchestra evoked rapturous responses. The box in which I was seated over the stage in the hall in Saint Paul was flooded with persons from the audience at the intermission before the beginning of the second half of the concert. The performance by Paul Freeman and the New York Philharmonic in 1977 induced an extraordinary stillness in Avery Fisher Hall for six seconds after the last notes could be heard. The applause that followed was like a loud thunderclap. I have never heard a response as loud and simultaneous after any other performance.

Performances of the entire String Quartet no. 1 have been rare. Joel Krosknick, cellist of the Juilliard String Quartet, offered to give the music to the student quartets that he coached. Arnold Steinhardt, violinist of the Guarneri String Quartet, voted against considering it with the other members of his group.

The String Quartet No. 2 has not fared much better. After listening to a tape of it on his car radio, the first violinist of the Manhattan String Quartet concluded fallaciously that it was typical of the expressionist style of the 1960s. He couldn't comprehend anything beyond Shostakovich.

I was fortunate in working with the Son Sonora String Quartet, an interracial ensemble comprised of experienced professional string players. Airi Yoshioka, Ashley Horne, violinists; Liuh-Wen Ting, violist; and Arash Amini are graduates of Juilliard or Curtis with acute sensibilities and dedication. In recording my two string quartets, an artistic level was reached that negated the need to contact any other ensembles. Tania Leon of the Brooklyn College music faculty was responsible for forming this group.

It is not unusual for persons to relate what they hear in a new work to what they can recall in a familiar work. One can understand why the average listener with no knowledge of anything technical in the music tries to make a connection between the new and the old. It is less understandable when a violinist in an orchestra remarks that my *Lyric for Strings* is reminiscent of the *Adagio for Strings* by Samuel Barber. The linear texture of the *Lyric*, the clearly defined structural components and the pizzicato, separates its conception from that of the earlier string work. The only thing that these two works have in common is the instrumentation. Performers whom one would expect to have some perspicacity after preparing a new work are generally inarticulate.

There had been two FM classical music stations in Chicago. When WNIB-FM was sold in 2001 and the music format was changed, Bruce Duffy, the host for the final program broadcasting classical music signed off by playing the *Lyric for Strings*. This work will always be associated with the demise of this radio station.

If Paul Kapp were alive today, he would have the satisfaction of knowing that my *Lyric for Strings*, which he published, is played more frequently than any other orchestral work by a living American composer. He had hoped to convince classical radio stations to use it as theme music for their programs. He could not have imagined that it would be performed regularly by major orchestras in this country, community and metropolitan orchestras, youth orchestras, and European orchestras.

SERENATA FOR CHAMBER ORCHESTRA

In the summer of 1984 the New York Philharmonic produced several concerts of contemporary music after the end of the subscription series. They were called Horizons '84. Before the summer concerts were initiated there was a panel discussion among music critics about American music. Raoul Abdul, critic for the *Amsterdam News*, a black publication, accused the panel of neglecting the music of black composers. Jacob Druckman decided to include one of my orchestral works in the festival. My Serenata for Chamber Orchestra was conducted by Gilbert Amy with the New York Philharmonic. This work had been commissioned by the Michigan Chamber Orchestra. Amy, a disciple of Boulez, had been brought to Yale by Druckman, who was the host for this series. The performance of the serenata suffered from Amy's ineptness as a conductor.

The Serenata for Chamber Orchestra resulted from a commission from a patron of the Michigan Chamber Orchestra in Detroit. Members of the orchestra suggested to George Pelham Head, a board member, that he could best retain the memory of his deceased wife with music to honor her. Head flew down to New Jersey to show me several albums of photos taken with her on their last European trip. It was a very affecting visit.

In the third movement of the serenata, I use quotes from "Tea for Two" and "As Time Goes By" from the movie *Casablanca*. "As Time Goes By" was composed by Herman Hupfeld, who was born in Montclair, New Jersey, and lived there most of his life. The guest conductor for the Michigan Chamber Orchestra played the premiere of the serenata rather poorly. There was a dinner after the concert. I sat at a table with George Pelham Head briefly. He appeared to be in a stupor. I was certain that the music meant nothing to him.

VIOLA SONATA

The idea of composing a chamber work for each of the string instruments was one that I had been harboring for a long time. When I realized that I was not interested in writing for the double bass, I decided to make a contribution to the viola repertoire.

My Sonata for Viola and Piano is in two movements. The number of movements was an intentional choice. The piano sonatas of Beethoven, op. 78 and op. 90, are works in which the second movement bears no relationship to the first movement. My decision to include material in the second movement that is similar to that in the first movement is a deviation from the norm. The term *sonata allegro* generally implies the use of sonata form in the first movement. This formal usage is employed with modification in the second movement of my Viola Sonata. The contrasting material returns in what is called the recapitulation in "sonata form" after reiterations (not a development) of the initial motive that occur in a middle section.

Several violists were contacted with the hope that they would be interested in playing the Viola Sonata. Recitals by these instrumentalists are relatively rare. The premiere of the sonata was given in Weill Hall, New York, in 1989 by Paul Neubauer. He also played it in Baltimore and Washington, DC. The emotional range of the work was only partially realized. The coda of the second movement introduces a fragment of the once popular "L'Homme Armé," a Renaissance song. This reference relates to a disturbing episode that traumatized my father when he returned to Washington, DC, after visiting my sister in New York. Our home was burglarized and his office was vandalized.

PAGEANT AND PROCLAMATION

The creation of a Performing Arts Center in Newark, New Jersey, was an effort made to revitalize the hub of a city that had experienced riots in the late 1960s. It also was intended to provide a new home for the New Jersey Symphony Orchestra. Lawrence Tamburri, the executive director of the orchestra, commissioned me to compose a work for the opening concert of the subscription series. Zdenek Macal, the conductor, programmed two works of Beethoven, the Lenore Overture no. 3 and the Ninth Symphony for the concert. My work, entitled *Pageant and Proclamation*, was sandwiched between the overture and the symphony.

Prudential Hall was jammed with an excited audience for this concert. Television cameras were hoisted on cranelike beams. The program was videotaped for PBS. *Pageant and Proclamation* concluded with a snippet from "When the Saints Go Marching In" and an extended quote of the spiritual "We Shall Overcome." The latter was chosen as a reference to the formidable social and economic problems of Newark, New Jersey.

A few weeks later, Tamburri invited me for lunch. In a restaurant in Montclair he told me that my commissioned work would not be included in the televised PBS program of the opening concert. No explanation was offered for the excision of my score. The televised program that viewers saw was an all-Beethoven program billed deceptively as the opening concert for the 1999–2000 season of the New Jersey Symphony.

Several years later Tamburri's ill-advised purchase of string instruments from a disreputable collector of Stradivari violins for the New Jersey Symphony saddled the orchestra with a huge debt. Under a barrage of heavy criticism for this investment in the future of the orchestra, Tamburri resigned from his position as executive director to become the CEO of the Pittsburgh Symphony. But the flak continued after his departure.

SUMMIT RECORDS

In 1999, I was asked to give a master class for composition students at Arizona State University in Phoenix. A program of my chamber works was presented when I was in residence there. The following evening, *Lilacs* was performed in a concert by the student orchestra in an auditorium designed by Frank Lloyd Wright. The conductor, Timothy Russell, engaged Faye Robinson, the soprano who had sung in the Boston Symphony premiere, for the solo part. She was on the voice faculty of the University of Arizona in Tucson.

I spoke to Russell about recording the concert performance of *Lilacs*. He volunteered to arrange a commercial recording session the day after the concert, and he enlisted the services of a recording engineer from Cleveland. I had discussed with Russell the possibility of including *Lilacs* on a CD with other works of mine. He had recorded some CDs in the past for Summit Records, a small local record label, and suggested that I consider this company.

Russell was also the conductor of the Columbus Pro Music Chamber Orchestra. I was offered a commission by that ensemble for a short work that the artistic administrator thought should herald the transition from the twentieth to the twenty-first century. The possibility of composing a work that would embody this unlikely scenario was further complicated by the administrator's notion that the score should become the exclusive property of the chamber orchestra. Unable to deal with this absurd contract, I asked the vice president of MMB, Douglas Jones, to sort out the quirkiness from this proposal. *Tangents for Orchestra* uses fragments from Cole Porter's "Night and Day" and Ellington's "I Let a Song Go Out of My Heart." The latter, encompassing three octaves in the cello part, is virtually unrecognizable.

LILACS CD RECORDING

The CD that I had contemplated would include the first commercially available recording of *Lilacs* as well as *Tangents*. (When I asked the Boston Symphony if I could purchase a copy of the premiere performance of *Lilacs* for a CD, I was told that the cost would be seventeen thousand dollars plus a fee for Ozawa and Faye Robinson.)

Two additional works were chosen to complete the CD. The engineer who recorded my String Quartet no. 2 in a festival in El Paso, Texas, sent me a cassette of that performance. The string quartet had two members of the Brentano String Quartet. I had several rehearsals with this ensemble when I was in El Paso. The concert performance was exceptionally good. The quality of the cassette was mediocre. The master tape had been damaged. But I had no choice in using the cassette copy.

The final work selected for the CD was my Violin and Piano Sonata no. 2. I had recorded it in my home with my son Gregory, who was more familiar with the work than I was. He had played it several times in public performances. The release of this CD by Summit Records has become an important document despite the poor intonation of the brass and woodwinds in *Tangents*. One of the culprits was a trumpet player hired as a last minute replacement for the recording. The recording engineer elected to use only two microphones to record *Tangents*. He was unable to effectively reproduce the timpani and percussion with this limited setup. The choice of the type of microphone was also inadvisable for the bright acoustic of the hall.

I had arrived in Columbus, Ohio, in the afternoon to attend the first rehearsal of *Tangents* by the Columbus Pro Musica Chamber Orchestra. It was scheduled for 7:00 p.m. that evening. I waited anxiously for someone from the orchestra to call me at my hotel about the location of the rehearsal. As the hour drew nigh, I was not contacted either by the new artistic administrator or by the conductor.

I heard *Tangents* for the first time in a preconcert rehearsal the next day. The failure to call me before the rehearsal was an embarrassing experience for Tim Russell and the artistic administrator. Amends were made when I was taken out to a late dinner in a good restaurant.

There were some disadvantages in working with Summit Records to produce the CD. This company spends very little money on advertising their recordings. Tim Russell advised me to use a publicist. Amy Blum, the woman whom he recommended, was quite knowledgeable, but she did nothing more than Albany Records would do routinely.

The agreement with Summit Records stated that I would receive a share of the CD sales. Four years elapsed without a penny from Harry Fox, the agency acting as a conduit for sales from Summit Records. After numerous phone calls and e-mails from my publisher and myself, Summit Records admitted that it had problems with its bookkeeping. Although I finally received a couple of hundred dollars, I will never know if there was more money that I should have received.

INDUCTIONS

My induction into the American Classical Music Hall of Fame in 2000 was very gratifying. I became the first living composer/pianist to receive this honor.

It has been difficult for me to judge the impact of my music after the early successes of my piano sonatas and trombone concerto. Comments about recordings of my music are made relatively infrequently, but too often by less than erudite persons. This is also true of the CDs of standard piano repertoire, works that I played when I was concertizing.

The plethora of wannabe music critics is evident not only in magazines like *Fanfare* and the *American Record Guide*, but on the Internet. Some of these reviewers fulfill their assignments responsibly. Others, like the editor of *Classics Today* who asserts that he can't distinguish between four completely different works of mine, lack both musical acumen and integrity.

The music critic for the *Newark Star-Ledger*, with a background in pop and rock, cannot conceal his limited capacity to discern quality in classical music. Without the ability to make judgments based on the knowledge of musical scores, these persons resort to comparative observations and to recycling the wealth of available biographical material. Reviews of recordings are generally based on the use of mid-fi playback equipment with limited resolution.

The induction ceremony was held in the Coolidge Auditorium of the Library of Congress in 2000. It was poorly publicized. Less than thirty-five persons, awardees included, were present. Medals suspended from long ribbons were conferred on the recipients from the stage. Only Leon Fleisher and myself were there. Beverly Sills was not. There was a short program of music. My *Prelude and Caprice* for piano was played after a Gottschalk solo piano work. A student ensemble from the Peabody Institute of Johns Hopkins University played the chamber version of Copland's *Appalachian Spring*. A buffet-styled lunch concluded the event. My son Gregory accompanied me to the presentation.

A year earlier, when I was honored by the American Academy of Arts and Letters, the induction ceremony was more elaborate. In attendance were recipients of various awards from all of the departments of the academy. A speech by an invited guest and photos taken of the assemblage extended the event into the late afternoon.

As Gregory and I were leaving the academy, Henry Louis Gates, who was also an inductee, spoke to us on the steps as we descended to the first floor. He remarked, "Not bad for a colored boy from West Virginia."

I reminded him that he had not responded to a letter that I sent to him regarding a lecture that I offered to give at Harvard University, where he was the chair of the Department of African and African American Studies. He said that he would look into it. I have heard nothing from him since that conversation. With the resignation of Eileen Southern from the Department of African and African American

Studies at Harvard, the last knowledgeable connection to black classical music was severed.

Two years after my induction, my son Gregory received a Charles Ives Fellowship from the American Academy.

CANVAS FOR WIND ENSEMBLE

When I was in Phoenix in 1999 as the composer-in-residence at Arizona State University, I received an invitation from Gary Hill, director of bands at the university, to have lunch with him. He had recently been appointed director of the College Band Association. During our conversation he proposed a commission for a band work that would include a setting of texts by prominent black leaders such as Dr. Martin Luther King or Bishop Tutu. Although I was interested in this project, I told Gary that I would prefer to write my own text for wind ensemble rather than for band. Numerous composers have written works using texts from the speeches of King. I preferred to use words that I had chosen.

Canvas for Wind Ensemble, Voices, and Chorus is divided into three movements. The movements are called extracts. They can be performed separately, although this is not recommended. "Extract I" is for wind ensemble. "Extract II" contains the text that I wrote for four male speakers and one female speaker. "Extract III" is a setting of Psalm 121 from the King James Bible for chorus.

The premiere of the work was given in 2001 by the North Texas Wind Ensemble and an a cappella choir from the music department of North Texas University. *Canvas* was recorded by Klavier Records for its series of contemporary works for band. All of the persons involved in the planning and performance of the commissioned work expressed their satisfaction with the unusual aspects of this work. For the average listener (reviewers included), the second extract seemed unfathomable, possibly because the text is not a continuous discourse and possibly because of the inclusion of a social commentary.

NETWORK FOR NEW MUSIC

A Philadelphia-based contemporary music ensemble, the Network for New Music, presented a concert of my music after I received the

Pulitzer Prize. It was given in the Art Alliance located several blocks south of the Curtis Institute of Music. The program included several of my songs and the Piano Sonata no. 2 played by Leon Bates, a native of Philadelphia.

When I was offered a commission for a chamber work by the Network for New Music, I composed a musical setting for a poem, "Abu Ben Adhem," written by an English poet, James Henry Leigh Hunt. The poem was derived from a historical account about an Arab king who renounced his authority to become a saint. This was one of several poems that many schoolchildren in Washington, DC, knew by heart.

The poem is recited in its entirety. An instrumental ensemble consisting of a flute, clarinet, bassoon, trumpet, trombone, piano, harp, violin, cello, and percussion provides a through-composed musical background. At the conclusion of the score there is a quote from a hymn composed by Alexander Reinagle, a German composer who settled in Philadelphia. The hymn, "In Christ There Is No East or West," was another favorite of my father.

CONNECTIONS

With the performances of my Sinfonia no. 3 in 2003, the Detroit Symphony extended its commitment to perform my music. In 1998 after I received a Koussevitzky Music Foundation Award, I sent the score of my Sinfonia no. 2 to the orchestra. Emil Kang, the CEO, contacted me a few weeks later to express his interest in programming the work. Neeme Jarvi conducted the premiere in 1999. When my Trombone Concerto received its first performance by the Detroit Symphony in 2000, I was awarded the first annual Classical Roots Award.

My Sinfonia no. 3 was not a commissioned work. When I called Kang in 2001 to tell him that I had finished another orchestral work, he requested the score. A few days later he told me that he had decided to schedule the premiere of the Sinfonia no. 3 for the following season. It was conducted by Andrey Boreyko. The audience responded enthusiastically to the work, although the conductor had some difficulty with the changing meters.

The Detroit Symphony has given many performances of my *Lyric for Strings* from the 1970s to the present. My Piano Concerto was recorded in Ford Auditorium for Columbia Records. I also played the

Tschaikowsky Piano Concerto no. 1 with the orchestra in the 1970s in an outdoor concert.

The Oberlin Conservatory Orchestra was the first ensemble to perform *Lilacs for Voice and Orchestra* after I received the Pulitzer Prize in Music. Soprano Daune Mahy, a professor of voice, was the soloist. The Conservatory Orchestra was conducted by Louis Lane, formerly the resident conductor of the Cleveland Orchestra. A conflict resulting from a previous commitment made it impossible for me to attend the performance of *Lilacs*.

A concert of my chamber music was given several days earlier. I was present for that occasion. The pianist for my Violin and Piano Sonata no. 2 was unable to cope with the difficulties in the music and faked most of her part. The violinist, Gregory Fulkerson, was not at his best.

My affiliation to the Eastman School of Music has remained remarkably strong since my graduation in 1956. I have returned to the school often to receive alumni awards and the Rochester Medal and to hear performances of my music. In 2006 the newly appointed director of the school, James Undercofler, commissioned me to write a work in a medium of my choice after I told him that I had just completed a score (*Canvas*) for wind ensemble and chorus.

The title of the commissioned work, *Foils for Orchestra (Hommage a Saint George)*, has several potential inferences. The most obvious image of "foils" is that of a fencing blade—the playful thrust of a weapon in the context of a sport or the use of a sword in a mortal combat between a warrior and a ferocious beast (Saint George and the dragon). Not too far-fetched is the connection of the title *Foils* to the Chevalier de Saint Georges, a black composer and swordsman.

A more generalized association with the title *Foils* could be contrived—a tense situation where there is conflict and confrontation, where force incites a counterforce as a deterrent of aggression. *Foils* was the second commission that I received from the Eastman School of Music. The initial octave, doubled, that begins the work suggests the thrust and penetration of a menacing weapon. *Foils* received its premiere at Eastman in October of 2006.

Although I received an honorary doctorate degree from the Curtis Institute of Music in 1997 when Gary Graffman was the director of the school, my music has not been performed there by students or by faculty since 1946. My *Lyric for Strings* was composed when I was a student at the Curtis Institute. Since that time, there has been no compunction to program my music. This neglect by the administration of the school and its faculty is mystifying. The current president, Roberto Diaz, who was considered a questionable choice from a viable field of candidates for the directorship, lacks the sensitivity to redress the issue.

The Juilliard School of Music, which I never attended, presented a "Perspective of the Music of George Walker" in 2006 that included a panel discussion hosted by its president, Joseph Polisi, with James DePreist of the conducting faculty. My piano trio, *Music for 3*, was performed on a Daniel Saidenberg Chamber Music series. The Juillard Orchestra, conducted by DePreist, also gave the New York premiere of my Sinfonia no. 3. But the contemporary music ensemble lead by Joel Sachs has not played any of my works.

The strongest connection that I have had in my home state of New Jersey has been with the Composers Guild of New Jersey. Robert Pollock, a fine pianist, composer, and the founder of the organization was living in South Jersey when we first met. He frequently arranged programs of contemporary music in various parts of the state and included some of my music on them. He also presented me in a solo piano recital that included my Piano Sonatas nos. 1 and 2 and the Beethoven Sonata op. 81a at the Noyes Museum in Oceanville, New Jersey. When he relocated to Maui in Hawaii, Robert invited me to participate in a series of contemporary music concerts there. I also gave a master class at the University of Hawaii. Robert selected me to become the honorary president of his organization, Ebb and Flow Arts.

Succeeding Robert Pollock as the director of the Composers Guild in New Jersey was William Anderson. Bill is a classical guitarist who is an adjunct faculty member of Sarah Lawrence College. About a year after my eightieth birthday, he rounded up enough support for a concert of my music at the Ethical Culture Society in New York. My son Gregory came from Colorado to New York to play my Sonata for Violin and Piano no. 1. This was the first time that we had played together in public. The other works on the program were my *Music for Brass (Sacred and Profane)*, the *T. S. Eliot Poem for Soprano and Chamber Ensemble*, the Piano Sonata no. 1, two songs ("And Wilt Thou Leave Me Thus" received a world premiere), and two organ works—*Improvisation on St. Theodulph* and *Spires*.

Shortly after I received the Pulitzer Prize in 1996 another organization, the New Jersey Chamber Music Society, a Montclair group, arranged a concert of my music at Bloomfield College in Bloomfield, New Jersey, a town adjacent to Montclair. I selected and rehearsed the soloists and ensembles for the concert. Afterward, President Noonan of Bloomfield College, who had made elaborate introductory remarks before the program began, suggested that he wanted to do something special for me. I was awarded an honorary doctorate at the next commencement.

MUSICAL QUARTERLY

The *Musical Quarterly* published in their fall 2000 issue an interview that I had with Mickey Thomas Terry. My collaboration with him was done to provide an accurate account of some of the details of my career. This format was somewhat unusual for this journal.

Leon Botstein, the editor of *Musical Quarterly*, asked one of his colleagues at Bard College, Ingrid Monson, to write a preface for the article. This was an unfortunate decision since Ms. Monson, a jazz study instructor, knew nothing about me or my music or black classical composers. This was evident in her original statements. Mickey requested that the preface be rewritten. Any number of classical music scholars could have been selected for the introductory statement. Botstein made no effort to find an appropriate choice.

VIOLIN CONCERTO

Since the conviction and musical comprehension manifested in the performances of my violin music by my son Gregory have not been fully acknowledged, I decided to compose a violin concerto for him. The paucity of concert-level black violinists makes it incumbent to have him introduce this work with a major orchestra in a major venue. He has always expended a great deal of care and intelligence in the preparation of my music and is not enticed, like some prominent instrumentalists and conductors, to skirt some of its difficulties or to alter it. Together, we could work on all aspects of this score to produce a reference performance.

My Violin Concerto does not contain the violinistic techniques found in the warhorses of the literature. Its demands are removed from the tedious repetitions of the minimalists and the cloying, *Wuthering Heights*-quality from some Hollywood-based composers.

When I was nearing its completion, I called my friend, Jim Undercofler. Jim, who had been appointed the director of the Eastman School of Music after Robert Freeman, had now become the CEO of the Philadelphia Orchestra. He asked me to send an early version of the score to him. A few months later I was told by an artistic administrator that the Philadelphia Orchestra was committed to having Gregory present the premiere of the Violin Concerto. There was also the possibility of having it played in Carnegie Hall. She informed me that Jessye Norman was curating a series of concerts in New York. The Philadelphia Orchestra, in one of its annual visits to the city, would be participating in that series.

There was a significant turn of events. I was told that Carnegie Hall was unwilling to have my son play the concerto in New York in March of 2009 with the Philadelphia Orchestra. The marketing mavens at Carnegie Hall wanted to cherry pick another soloist. A Tchaikowsky Competition Prize winner was being considered.

I wrote to Jessye Norman to inform her about the singular opportunity that this concerto offered for her series and to tell her about the significance of the father-son relationship in the creation of the work. She didn't respond to my letters. Then I learned that she was responsible for the proposal to select another soloist for the Violin Concerto.

Jim Undercofler was disturbed by what appeared to be the intransigence of the Carnegie Hall administrators. After I told him that I would not agree to have the premiere played by another soloist, Jim very generously rescheduled the concerto so that Gregory could give the premiere with the Philadelphia Orchestra in December of 2009.

Charles Dutoit, who had been engaged to conduct the Violin Concerto, agreed to substitute *Lilacs* in place of the concerto for the Carnegie Hall program. When Carnegie Hall balked at paying for the soloist in *Lilacs*, the Philadelphia Orchestra extracted the fee for the soloist out of its budget. Russell Thomas, a tenor, was selected for three performances in Philadelphia and a single concert in Carnegie Hall.

Lilacs *sheet music from Carnegie Hall performance, March 2009*

This would be the first time that the work that was originally composed for a tenor would be sung by one.

DA CAMERA

In January of 2008 I was contacted by a violinist from a chamber ensemble called Musica Reginae. It is based in Queens, New York. It would appear that the choice of the title for their trio, when translated from the Latin, refers to their home base. I was commissioned to compose a work for a piano trio and a string orchestra. I also added harp, celesta, and percussion to the score.

Da Camera was supposed to have its premiere in Carnegie Hall with the New Haven Symphony in February of 2009. The score contains optional string parts for a student orchestra from the Amistad Academy in New Haven, which the conductor, William Boughton, insisted upon having as participants in the performance.

Musica Reginae was unable to pay for the rental of Carnegie Hall. A performance in New Haven of the commissioned work by the New Haven Symphony was cancelled. The student ensemble never materialized. The date and venue for the premiere remain undetermined. The work is in limbo.

Da Camera is a composition in one movement. The piano trio is integrated into the fabric of the string orchestra part as soloists rather than as an ensemble. Toward the end of the work four quotes that include a Broadway tune, a spiritual, and two jazz standards are incorporated.

A DIFFERENT CHALLENGE

The long driveway that slopes gently down to a two-car garage that I share with a neighbor is lined on my side with rhododendrons and on his side with nondescript bushes with branches randomly poking out over the tarred surface. The summer of 2003 had scarcely begun when I noticed a single tomato plant growing in a small grassless area adjacent to the corner of his side of the garage. Several weeks later, when fully ripened tomatoes dangled from their stems, I congratulated Reggie on his successful implantation. He offered me three tomatoes that were quite tasty. The following spring I decided to grow my own tomatoes.

I have never forgotten an incident at Cousin Lila's home in Virginia when a slightly older relative, a girl, had plucked from a leafy plot of vegetables beside a dirt road leading to the main highway a perfectly spherical red tomato, warm from the afternoon sun, and given it to me. I could not have imagined a vegetable so succulent that the addition of sugar would have been an affront to its naturalness.

In March of 2004 I purchased two tomato plants from a garden center in West Caldwell, New Jersey. Digging into soil a few feet from the steps leading to the back door of my house, I was chagrined to discovered that layers of cinders had been dumped there by a previous owner who had heated the house with coal. Cleaning out two ten-inch holes was not a cure-all solution. But I proceeded to prepare them for the planting.

Only one of the two bushes was productive. I watched a green tomato grow large before beginning to turn red. I surmised that after a few more days the color change would be complete. The tomato would make a delicious salad.

Two days later when I went outside to water the plants, I was shocked to find that the tomato was missing. There were no bits or pieces of it to suggest that it had been partially devoured. Neither the possum in the neighborhood or the family of skunks spotted crossing Grove Street on a warmish evening could be suspected.

The most logical intruder might have been the meter reader for the gas company who always knocked politely on the back door. A wave of disbelief left me distraught as I began to consider all possibilities. My anger increased as I became convinced that this was indeed a theft. Inquiries were made to the residents on my block, but the mystery of the disappearance of the tomato was never solved.

Nevertheless, I was encouraged by this partial success. The following spring I bought five tomato plants, placing them in a sunny area by the hedges at the entrance of the backyard. The clay deposits in the soil were worrisome. Aluminum foil was placed at ground level above the roots to protect the plants against cutworms. Topsoil, grass clippings, egg shells, and dehydrated manure were liberally applied to counter the mineral deficiency in the soil.

All of the five plants flourished. The yield was unflagging from mid-July and August until the end of September. The Ramapo hybrid beefsteak tomato was large, red, juicy, sweet, and thin skinned. I had not expected an abundance of this proportion. There were far too many tomatoes on my kitchen table to be enjoyed by one person.

My neighbors became the first recipients of my largesse. After bringing two bags of tomatoes to the local food pantry, I was dubbed "the tomato man" with my next appearance. For many home growers in the area, tomato plants in their gardens that summer, after a wet spring, had not fared well. Arriving at the shelter as food was being packaged for delivery, I was a welcomed contributor to their resources. The Montclair Senior Care Center and the YWCA became my next targets for the disposition of this excess.

It became difficult to think of more individuals who might be interested in consuming some of these wholesome specimens. The editor and the assistant editor of the *Montclair Times*, a composer living in the next block down the street from me, and Daisy, Henry Booker's older sister who had been living in Montclair before I arrived, were the next recipients.

I drove to New York to leave a bag with the doorman at Walter Hautzig's apartment building. When I went to visit my son Gregory in Colorado, I brought him several of my most impressive ones. He was incredulous when I told him that I had grown them. A box sent to my son Ian in San Francisco lay undiscovered until it was too late for them to be edible. Large ones were given to a young couple, Colleen and Matt, who had invited me to their apartment for a Thanksgiving dinner.

Sal, with whom I frequently played tennis, was a driver for the DeCamp Bus Line that transported New Jerseyans back and forth to New York. His bus route took him past my home every day. I asked him if he wanted some choice tomatoes. We agreed to meet the next day so that he could pick them up. At the designated time, he stopped his bus in front of my house. I ran outside and handed him two sizable brown paper bags of my produce. I could have created a roadside stand on Grove Street for several days with the batch that remained.

When I did not immediately receive the compliments that I expected, I called my friends to elicit a flattering opinion of my donation. My tomatoes were better than those sold on Saturdays at the farmers market in Montclair. I thought that their distinction would be appreciated. But the comments that I received were, for the most part, perfunctory.

Daisy had already told me that she preferred stewing her tomatoes. (The flavor of my tomatoes was special when they were sliced.) Several months later, Sal admitted that he really didn't like tomatoes. I had incorrectly assumed that because he was Italian, he would relish them.

I never experienced the quantity and quality of this cornucopia in subsequent years. With some reluctance I decided to limit my agricultural efforts to nurturing only two plants each spring.

· 7 ·

Ruminations

*H*aving two sons who are intensely involved in the arts has enabled me to communicate with exceptionally conversant persons who can now begin to relate to my experiences. My younger son, Ian, is a gifted playwright whose objective with the theater company that he cofounded is to project an awareness of the social issues that he considers important. His productions in San Francisco offer premieres of his own works as well as productions by other playwrights.

In my effort to create substantial works that have a strong musical profile and an elegance of construction, I have attempted to contribute something unique to the repertoire of various genres and to dispel the latent belief that a black composer is incapable of producing music that extends beyond a racial divide.

Several important works have not been funded. A work that has not been commissioned requires a considerable effort on the part of the composer to find performers and ensembles who are willing to program it. This is not an uncommon situation. Every artist is obliged to find avenues and opportunities that will enable him or her to be heard or seen.

The effort to create visibility can be expensive when no financial support is available from organizations that are created to foster the arts. The difficulty of getting orchestral music recorded in the United States has resulted in composers seeking cheaper possibilities in Europe and in Russia. But the weakened American dollar and the strength of the euro and the English pound have made recording outside of the United States more costly now.

It was important for me to make a CD of some of my orchestral music that was representative of several different musical conceptions. I arranged to have five of my works recorded in Poland. The projected budget was exceeded when outdated parts sent by my publisher, MMB Music, to the Sinfonia Varsovia in Warsaw were held in customs for incomplete paperwork. When the correct parts were finally shipped, there was inadequate preparation for the recording of my *Address for Orchestra*.

My Sinfonia no. 1 that was premiered at Tanglewood and dismissed in a review by John Rockwell can now be recognized on this CD for its individuality and power. This work had not been performed since its premiere by the student group in Lenox, Massachusetts. *Overture: In Praise of Folly* and *Hoopla (A Touch of Glee)* were also included on this CD, which is titled *George Walker: Great American Orchestral Works, Vol. 1.* The conductor was Ian Hobson.

An application for a partial reimbursement for the works that were recorded in Poland was rejected by the Copland Fund. When I requested an explanation for the rejection, the director, James Kendrick, absolved the awards committee of dereliction and insensitivity and offered a predictably doleful excuse—there was insufficient funding for all meritorious projects.

The mystery of creation is imbedded in every good composition. I find satisfaction in manipulating materials, in hewing to formal concepts, and in making allusions to other music that may appear irrelevant in the context of the score. When these references are successfully incorporated, they are seamlessly inclusive.

Ideas that can captivate the listener are illusive. A composer cannot predict the kind of reception that a new composition will get. The importance of simple intervallic relationships, the frequencies of two notes played successively or simultaneously cannot be underestimated. Heard as varying degrees of tension and existing as an expressive potential this tangency exerts an entrancing power that never ceases to amaze me. Care in the choice of these and more complex relationships requires a scrutiny that should be exercised as much in contemporary music as it has been in the music of earlier periods.

The quality of a performance may be less reliable in determining the intrinsic qualities of a new work than one might suppose. It is almost a misconception to assume that a good performance of an intricate work will make it easier to evaluate. There is often much that has not been discerned and much that must be grasped quickly. But there are always details that have a passing significance.

The composer will be pleased to hear what he wrote if the performance is good. On the other hand, a work heard for the first time by most listeners generally leaves a superficial impression. A more definitive impression can occur if it is reinforced by additional listening—which may not happen. If it does, the listener's taste or even his mood will determine if the impression is sustained.

The first rehearsal of a new work is, for me, as important as its first performance. There is an underlying sense of anticipation and, with it, a sense of uncertainty—like entering a room in which many of the arranged items are not completely recognizable. The composer cannot be certain of what will happen to cause some consternation. By reviewing the score before a rehearsal, he can prepare himself to hear what he has written and to recall decisions that were made in composing the work. But if a horn player raises his hand after the orchestra has stopped and the conductor turns around to seek clarification from the composer, disquietude can erode composure.

I have always been inclined to downplay the importance of inspiration, a notion typically entertained by laypersons in the creation of any art. The sudden illuminating flash as a compelling impetus to create has seldom appeared in my consciousness. Nevertheless, I can imagine that there are artists who do experience this mystical stimulus, a perception realized through sight, sound, or thinking that can trigger a strong response. Perception, however, will not induce every artist to respond to the stimulus with the same compulsion. I am more inclined to question the validity of the disclosure.

Will is a stronger and more consistent factor in energizing the intent to create. The beginning of a new work is consequential. It demands the most careful preparation. Refining and reshaping initial ideas become essential in providing the key that opens the door to a dimly lit vista. From that point one can perceive possibilities that will affect the direction, character, and momentum of the work.

The exception to my temperamental disinclination to the phenomenon of inspiration occurred when I was mulling over the beginning of *Pageant and Proclamation*, commissioned by the New Jersey Symphony for the opening concert of the New Jersey Performing Arts Center. I was taking a shower in the morning when I began to sing five notes, B–F#–G–E–A. The symmetry of these notes was immediately apparent to me. After notating them, I experimented with other pitch possibilities.

I could not find anything better to serve as the principal motive in the work. These notes came unsought, like manna from heaven.

In my efforts to make the black classical composer more visible in a sea of ignorance and indifference, certain particulars have emerged that reflect attitudes existing in society in general.

There are many individuals who have retained a stereotypical view of the home environment of a black person. A remark made by a nurse in Mountainside Hospital in Montclair where I was having a checkup exemplifies this. She told me in a friendly tone as she left my room that I could find the Bill Cosby program on television by using my remote and added, "Of course, they are not your typical family."

There is also the deeply imbedded assumption that I, a black concert pianist, should play jazz as well. These assumptions have been voiced on different occasions by many persons—Caucasians, Asians, remarkable musicians such as Serkin and Boulanger, and well-meaning concert goers. The thought has never occurred to them that this notion jibes with their visualization of the black ghetto.

No matter how much traditional training in classical music a black artist has absorbed, there's the underlying suspicion for some that his native habitat is the realm of jazz. A New York music critic could find little to comment on after a performance of my Cello Sonata in Weill Hall other than to mention a brief jazzy section in the third movement. The fugue was beyond his cognizance. All too often a less than subtle depreciation of the intellectual capabilities and sensibilities of black persons are manifest.

When I was asked to write an article on the black composer for the Sunday edition of the *New York Times*, I was assured of being able to use about fifteen hundred words. Two days before the publication's deadline, I received a note accompanying the faxed proof from the editor. He apologized for the reduction of the word count. The proof revealed other changes. He had substituted "mulatto," a word that I detest, for "a man of colour," which I had used to describe an attendant in an auto wash whose ethnic background was unclear to me. The excuse that the editor gave for his usage was that his newspaper was now encouraging a more colloquial style.

In the liner notes of one of my CDs, I expressed my admiration for the technique of thematic transformation employed by Liszt in his tone poems. The music assumes a character markedly different from the original material by altering the rhythm. The allusive content of the music is clearly affected by the change in note values. I used this example to refute an observation made by Stravinsky in his Poetics of Music, lectures which he gave at Harvard. He stated that music cannot express anything.

One can agree that an emotion felt after listening to a specific piece of music can be difficult to describe. It is certainly subjective. It can be suggestive rather than definitive. To declare that music is impotent is a misguided statement even if it was made by a great composer. One can extrapolate that if Stravinsky believed this assertion, it may have been made to distance himself from the proclivity evident in his earlier scores.

Neoclassicism was a direction taken by composers seeking an escape from romanticism and impressionism. It involves a sorting out of effects from the classical period. The results from talentless composers can be emasculatory and sterile. Too many composers have imitated the creators of neoclassical works. In Stravinsky's case and that of Hindemith, the rhythmic and melodic preferences that define their signature are more dominant than their extractions from the baroque or Viennese classical period.

Abstraction can be achieved in other arts, but not in music. Sound is produced from vibration. Vibrations are felt.

A retired doctor (perhaps a bone-cracking chiropractor) cum music guru, in a review of the aforementioned CD on Amazon.com, objected to what he considered to be my depreciation of Stravinsky. This was done, according to him, to boost my importance as a composer. What his comments revealed was a resistance to a rational rebuttal, one that has validity. It is an opinion at odds with the genuflection accorded famous personalities. (They can't be wrong.) But the kernel needs to be separated from the husk.

BLACK COMPOSERS

In the first lecture sponsored by UNISYS and the Detroit Symphony, I spoke about the difficulties that black composers have in getting their music performed. I concluded the talk by expressing a limited optimism about their future prospects. A critic from the *New York Times* attended the second lecture of this series. In an article in this newspaper, he remarked that the bitter tone of the first lecture was absent in the talk given by another composer. Obviously, he did not choose to weigh all of the comments that I made.

The surfacing of an unwarranted and sometimes venomous attitude in classical music circles mirrors the animus found in other professions. Facts are resented if they offer a contradictory view. In this case, there was a good reason for dissatisfaction. The status quo will never be acceptable as long as there is a limit placed on opportunities. The double standard that is synonymous with prejudicial opinions is concealed in pseudorational statements.

The history of music is littered with remarks made by obtuse critics to ridicule certain works. Their comments affect an appreciation of the true value of a work. This may take years to emerge. A few composers have been equally demeaning in their attacks on other composers. These remarks are tucked away by musicologists as if they have some meaningful importance.

Since there are numerous instances of unbridled and undeserved criticism, the question "Why should contemporary black classical composers be treated any differently?" may be asked. For an answer to this it is essential to acknowledge first that the criticism received by well-trained contemporary black composers can be more consistently subtractive than the comments that other composers receive.

A twenty-first-century book, *Classical Music in America* by Joseph Horowitz, containing only a passing reference to William Grant Still, typifies the continued neglect of black composers by recent historians. The book's bibliography does not even include the landmark volume by Eileen Southern *The Music of Black Americans.*

Similar criticism was leveled at *Soundings*, published by Glenn Watkins twenty years earlier. His book, subtitled "Music in the Twentieth Century," has a detailed discussion of composers who have used jazz. But there is no mention of Duke Ellington. All of those referenced were white composers. It should also be noted that there are no orchestration textbooks that contain examples from scores by black composers. For these authors, their music does not exist. These omissions undermine progress toward inclusiveness.

The respected musicologist Alfred Einstein, who taught at Smith College, published a book entitled *Music in the Romantic Era.* In a chapter on nationalism in North America, he makes egregious statements that are embarrassingly wrongheaded in associating "Old Folks at Home" and "My Kentucky Home" with spirituals. In calling spirituals "creative imitations of European impulses," Einstein disqualifies himself as a scholar in the area of folk music. It is all too apparent that there was no effort on his part to research this trove of material that is woven into the social fabric of our country.

Statements released as facts can be difficult to repudiate. There is nothing that has occurred in the beginning of my career as a composer/pianist that can connect me to the Harlem Renaissance. I have not known any of the major poets or painters who have been associated with that period nor have I discussed this milieu with anyone at any time. My focus in classical music has followed a completely divergent path from that of black artists in other fields.

Hale Smith told me that at the conclusion of his *Ritual and Incantations*, an orchestral work performed in Carnegie Hall, another composer who was sitting in the box with him touched his arm and said, "That was awesome." The review that appeared in one newspaper dismissed the work as little more than garbage.

Ritual and Incantations is one of the most suspenseful works imaginable. Its tension is greater even than the atmosphere evoked in parts of Stravinsky's *Le Sacre du Printemps*. It is inconceivable to me that anyone could react so negatively to this music. The hostility expressed in this review clearly has personal and probably racial overtones.

This same attitude that is reductive in nature appears to stem from the supposition that a European lineage automatically imparts authority and insight, and, hence, a certain superiority. This justifies the dismissal of works by persons who, because of their ethnicity, could not possibly be capable of originality. But talent and intelligence are not exclusively apportioned to any ethnic group, nationality, or social class.

The visibility of black classical performers, composers, and conductors has increased significantly. Black artists who have achieved international stature have shown as little interest in performing the works of contemporary black classical composers as their white counterparts. Black conductors, with the exception of James DePreist, have been content to play my *Lyric for Strings* because its effect is virtually guaranteed. They have shown no compulsion to program any of the works for full orchestra. (Tokenism can exist without racist implications.) The emergence of black chamber ensembles like the Ritz Chamber Players that

Left to right: Grayson, Lori, Dashiel, and Gregory Walker

are capable of a very high caliber of performance are a welcome addition to the concert circuit.

Avoiding works from contemporary composers is the road that highly esteemed black singers (Shirley Verrett, Kathleen Battle, Leontyne Price, and Jessye Norman, among many others) and the pianist Andre Watts have paved to maintain their success. Their acclaim, emanating in some cases from *Porgy and Bess* or Virgil Thomson's *Four Saints in Three Acts*, is perpetuated by concentrating on the repetition of standard repertoire and the resurrection of spirituals.

Opportunities for aspiring young black pianists may seem to be unlimited at first. When they diminish, Gershwin's *Rhapsody in Blue* is one of their most viable choices for maintaining a semblance of musical activity.

My impression of this work has not changed since I heard it for the first time as a freshman at Oberlin College. The parallelism of chords, the sequences, the repetitions, and the rather maudlin melody of the middle section instinctively affected my impression of its worth. When I was on the roster of the National Concert Artists, an audition was arranged for me with one of the conductors for the Grant Parks Concerts in Chicago. After the audition, the conductor offered me an engagement to play the *Rhapsody in Blue*. When I suggested another concerto, he became silent and the conversation ended. I did not receive a contract for an appearance the following summer.

My mother's admonition to accept the bad with the good presents a formidable challenge—that of maintaining an equilibrium. But it is admirable advice. Remembering the help of strangers who become friends and advocates gives one pause in the exceedingly steep climb toward recognition and acceptance. The unexpected dots the path with rewards that could not be anticipated and provides moments of pleasure, if only briefly experienced, and satisfaction that comes with a backward glance down the precipitous slope at the distance already covered. Remembering the lives of those who have preceded me and those of my parents—hoisting with great concern and pride a curious boy undaunted by the possibility of rejection on their shoulders—has been the focus of this book. They deserve the approbation for the measure of success that I have achieved.

Appendix A: Discography

GEORGE WALKER

George Walker: A Portrait (Albany Records, 1994)
Five Fancies for Clarinet and Piano Four Hands
George Walker, composer
Eric Thomas, clarinet
Vivian Taylor and John McDonald, piano
Antifonys for Chamber Orchestra
George Walker, composer
Royal Philharmonic Orchestra
Paul Freeman, conductor
An Eastman Overture
George Walker, composer
Eastman Philharmonia
David Effron, conductor
Variations for Orchestra
George Walker, composer
New Philharmonia Orchestra
Paul Freeman, conductor
Cantata for Soprano, Tenor, Boys Choir, and Chamber Orchestra
George Walker, composer
Joyce Mathis, soprano
Walter Turnbull, tenor
Boys Choir of Harlem
Orchestra of St. Luke's
Warren Wilson, conductor

Three Pieces for Organ
George Walker, composer
Mickey Terry, organ

George Walker in Recital (Albany Records, 1994)
Moment Musical, op. 94
Franz Schubert, composer
George Walker, piano
Barcarolle, op. 60
Frederic Chopin, composer
George Walker, piano
Sonata no. 1
George Walker, composer
George Walker, piano
Mazurka, op. 63, no. 2
Frederic Chopin, composer
George Walker, piano
Waltz, op. 39, no. 15
Johannes Brahms, composer
George Walker, piano
Sonata in B-flat Major, L. 39
Domenico Scarlatti, composer
George Walker, piano
Sonata in D Minor, L. 366
Domenico Scarlatti, composer
George Walker, piano
Sonata in E Major, L. 430
Domenico Scarlatti, composer
George Walker, piano
Sonata in G Major, L. 490
Domenico Scarlatti, composer
George Walker, piano
Sonata in E Major, L. 23
Domenico Scarlatti, composer
George Walker, piano
Sonata in A Major, L. 23
Domenico Scarlatti, composer
George Walker, piano

Sonata no. 26, op. 81a
> Ludwig Van Beethoven, composer
> George Walker, piano

George Walker: Chamber Music (Albany Records, 1996)

Piano Sonata no. 2
> George Walker, composer
> George Walker, piano

Sonata for Cello and Piano
> George Walker, composer
> Italo Babini, cello
> George Walker, piano

Poem for Soprano and Chamber Ensemble
> George Walker, composer
> Capitol Chamber Artists
> Angelo Frascarelli, conductor
> Ian Walker, speaker

Sonata for Violin and Piano no. 1
> George Walker, composer
> Gregory Walker, violin
> George Walker, piano

Music for Brass (Sacred and Profane)
> George Walker, composer
> American Brass Quintet

The Music of George Walker (Composer Recordings, Inc., 1997)

Piano Sonata no. 2
> George Walker, composer
> George Walker, piano

Spatials for Piano
> George Walker, composer
> George Walker, piano

Spektra for Piano
> George Walker, composer
> George Walker, piano

Sonata for Violin and Piano no. 1
> George Walker, composer
> Gregory Walker, violin
> George Walker, piano

Prelude and Caprice for Piano
    George Walker, composer
    George Walker, piano
Songs
    George Walker, composer
    Phyllis Bryn-Julson, soprano
    George Walker, piano
Variations for Piano
    George Walker, composer
    George Walker, piano

George Walker, Winner of the 1996 Pulitzer Prize in Music (Albany Records, 1997)
    Prelude and Fugue in D Major, WTC no. 5
        J. S. Bach, composer
        George Walker, piano
    Kreisleriana, op. 16
        Robert Schumann, composer
        George Walker, piano
    Étude in C-sharp Minor, op. 10, no. 4
        Frederic Chopin, composer
        George Walker, piano
    Étude in G-flat Major, op. 10, no. 5
        Frederic Chopin, composer
        George Walker, piano
    Étude in E-flat Minor, op. 10, no. 6
        Frederic Chopin, composer
        George Walker, piano
    Étude in B Minor, op. 25, no. 10
        Frederic Chopin, composer
        George Walker, piano
    Nocturne in F-sharp Major, op. 15, no. 2
        Frederic Chopin, composer
        George Walker, piano
    Toccata
        Francis Poulenc, composer
        George Walker, piano

George Walker: Orchestral Works (Albany Records, 1998)

    Serenata for Chamber Orchestra
        George Walker, composer
        Cleveland Chamber Symphony
        Edwin London, conductor
    Lyric for Strings
        George Walker, composer
        Cleveland Chamber Symphony
        Edwin London, conductor
        Gregory Walker, violin
    Poeme for Violin and Orchestra
        George Walker, composer
        Cleveland Chamber Symphony
        Edwin London, conductor
        William Demsey, narrator
        Eileen Moore, soprano
    Orpheus for Chamber Orchestra
        George Walker, composer
        Cleveland Chamber Symphony
        Edwin London, conductor
    Folk Songs for Orchestra
        George Walker, composer
        Cleveland Chamber Symphony
        Edwin London, conductor

Lilacs: The Music of George Walker (Summit Records, 2000)

    Tangents for Chamber Orchestra
        George Walker, composer
    Lilacs for Voice and Orchestra
        George Walker, composer
        Arizona State University Symphony Orchestra
        Faye Robinson, soprano
    Wind Set for Woodwind Quintet
        George Walker, composer
        Peggy Schecter, flute
        Jerome Ashby, horn

Sonata for Violin and Piano no. 2
   George Walker, composer
   Gregory Walker, violin
   George Walker, piano
String Quartet no. 2
   George Walker, composer

George Walker: American Virtuoso (Albany Records, 2001)
Sonata in C Minor, Hob. XVI/20
   Franz Josef Haydn, composer
   George Walker, piano
Sonata in E-flat Major, K. 282
   Wolfgang Amadeus Mozart, composer
   George Walker, piano
Impromptu in A-flat Major, op. 90, no. 4
   Franz Schubert, composer
   George Walker, piano
Nocturne in D-flat Major, op. 27, no. 2
   Frederic Chopin, composer
   George Walker, piano
Mazurka in F Minor, op. 63, no. 2
   Frederic Chopin, composer
   George Walker, piano
Mazurka in C Major, op. 33, no. 3
   Frederic Chopin, composer
   George Walker, piano
Mazurka in D-flat Major, op. 30, no. 3
   Frederic Chopin, composer
   George Walker, piano
Étude in G-flat Major, op. 10, no. 5
   Frederic Chopin, composer
   George Walker, piano
Bruyères (Prelude no. 5, Bk. 11)
   Claude Debussy, composer
   George Walker, piano
Valse Oubliée
   Franz Liszt, composer
   George Walker, piano

Funerailles
 Franz Liszt, composer
 George Walker, piano

George Walker in Concert (Albany Records, 2002)
 Fantasia in C, op. 17
  Robert Schumann, composer
  George Walker, piano
 La Puerta del Vino
  Claude Debussy, composer
  George Walker, piano
 Bruyères
  Claude Debussy, composer
  George Walker, piano
 General Lavine Eccentric
  Claude Debussy, composer
  George Walker, piano
 Prelude and Caprice
  George Walker, composer
  George Walker, piano
 Prelude in G, op. 32, no. 5
  Serge Rachmaninoff, composer
  George Walker, piano
 Ballade in F Minor, op. 52
  Frederic Chopin, composer
  George Walker, piano
 Polonaise in A Flat Major, op. 53
  Frederic Chopin, composer
  George Walker, piano

George Walker (Albany Records, 2005)
 In Time of Silver Rain
  George Walker, composer
  Patricia Green, mezzo-soprano
  George Walker, piano
 I Never Saw a Moor
  George Walker, composer

Patricia Green, mezzo-soprano
George Walker, piano
Mother Goose
George Walker, composer
Patricia Green, mezzo-soprano
George Walker, piano
Response
George Walker, composer
Patricia Green, mezzo-soprano
George Walker, piano
Softly, Blow Lightly
George Walker, composer
Patricia Green, mezzo-soprano
George Walker, piano
Wild Nights
George Walker, composer
Patricia Green, mezzo-soprano
George Walker, piano
Mary Wore Three Links of Chain
George Walker, composer
Patricia Green, mezzo-soprano
George Walker, piano
Modus for Chamber Ensemble
George Walker, composer
Tara O'Connor, flute
Robert Ingliss, oboe
William Anderson, guitar
Oren Fader, guitar
Calvin Wiersma, violin
Susannah Chapman, cello
Sonetto del Petrarca 104
Franz Liszt, composer
George Walker, piano
Valse Oubliée no. 1
Franz Liszt, composer
George Walker, piano
Mazurka in C, op. 33, no. 2
Frederic Chopin, composer
George Walker, piano

Mazurka in D-flat, op. 30, no. 3
    Frederic Chopin, composer
    George Walker, piano
Mazurka in F Minor, op. 63, no. 2
    Frederic Chopin, composer
    George Walker, piano
Étude in G-flat, op. 10, no. 5
    Frederic Chopin, composer
    George Walker, piano
Scherzo in E, op. 54
    Frederic Chopin, composer
    George Walker, piano
Prayer
    George Walker, composer
    Trent Johnson, organ
Improvisation on St. Theodulph
    George Walker, composer
    Trent Johnson, organ
Spires
    George Walker, composer
    Trent Johnson, organ

George Walker: 60th Anniversary Retrospective (Albany Records, 2006)
    Lyric for Strings
        George Walker, composer
        Son Sonora String Quartet
    Perimeters for Clarinet and Piano
        George Walker, composer
        Scott Anderson, clarinet
        Robert Pollock, piano
    Piano Sonata in B Minor
        Franz Liszt, composer
        George Walker, piano
    Canvas for Wind Ensemble, Voices and Chorus
        George Walker, composer
        North Texas Wind Symphony and A Cappella Choir
        Eugene Corporon, conductor
        Jonathan Howell, tenor

George Walker: Great American Orchestral Works, Vol. 1 (Albany Records, 2008)
>Address for Orchestra
>>George Walker, composer
>>Sinfonia Varsovia
>>Ian Hobson, conductor
>
>Overture: In Praise of Folly
>>George Walker, composer
>>Sinfonia Varsovia
>>Ian Hobson, conductor
>
>Sinfonia no. 1
>>George Walker, composer
>>Sinfonia Varsovia
>>Ian Hobson, conductor
>
>Sinfonia no. 3
>>George Walker, composer
>>Sinfonia Varsovia
>>Ian Hobson, conductor
>
>Hoopla (A Touch of Glee)
>>George Walker, composer
>>Sinfonia Varsovia
>>Ian Hobson, conductor

George Walker: Great American Chamber Music (Albany Records, 2009)
>String Quartet no. 1
>>George Walker, composer
>>Son Sonora String Quartet
>
>String Quartet no. 2
>>George Walker, composer
>>Son Sonora String Quartet
>
>Piano Sonata no. 4
>>George Walker, composer
>>Frederick Moyer, piano
>
>Songs
>>George Walker, composer
>>James Martin, baritone
>>George Walker, piano

OTHER ARTISTS AND COMPILATIONS

Frederick Moyer (GM Recordings, 1985)
Piano Sonata no. 4
George Walker, composer
Frederick Moyer, piano

Piano Music by African American Composers (Composers Recordings, Inc., 1993)
Piano Sonata no. 1
George Walker, composer
Natalie Hinderas, piano

American Trombone Concertos (Bis, 1993)
Concerto for Trombone and Orchestra
George Walker, composer
Malmö Symphony Orchestra
James DePriest, conductor
Christian Lindberg, trombone

The Composer-Performer: 40th Anniversary (Composers Recordings, Inc., 1994)
Spatials for Piano
George Walker, composer
George Walker, piano

Lilacs for Voice and Orchestra: The Music of George Walker (Summit Records, 2000)
Tangents for Chamber Orchestra
George Walker, composer
Pro Musica Chamber Orchestra of Columbus, Ohio
Timothy Russell, conductor
Lilacs for Voice and Orchestra
Faye Robinson, soprano
Arizona State University Orchestra
Timothy Russell, conductor
Wind Set for Woodwind Quintet
Sonata for Violin and Piano no. 2

Gregory Walker, violin
George Walker, piano
String Quartet no. 2
El Paso String Quartet

Time Pieces (Klavier, 2001)
Canvas for Speaking Voices, Two Solo Tenors, Chorus, and Orchestra
George Walker, composer
North Texas Wind Symphony
Eugene Corporon, conductor

Black Composers Series (Royce Music, 2002)
Piano Concerto
George Walker, composer
Detroit Symphony Orchestra
Paul Freeman, conductor
Natalie Hinderas, piano

Appendix B: Major Compositions

Abu for Narrator and Chamber Ensembles *
Address for Orchestra
Antifonys for Chamber Orchestra
Cantata for Soprano, Tenor, Boys Choir, and Chamber Orchestra *
Canvas for Wind Ensemble, Speakers, and Chorus *
Concerto for Cello and Orchestra *
Concerto for Piano and Orchestra *
Dialogus for Cello and Orchestra *
An Eastman Overture *
Emily Dickinson Songs *
Five Fancies for Clarinet and Piano Four Hands *
Foils for Orchestra *
Folk Songs for Orchestra
Guido's Hand for Piano *
Hoopla for Orchestra *
Lilacs for Voice and Orchestra *
Lyric for Strings
Mass for Soloists, Chorus, Organ, and Orchestra *
Modus for Two Guitars and Chamber Ensemble *
Music for 3 *
Music for Brass (Sacred and Profane) *
Music for Two Pianos *
Nine Songs for Voice and Piano
Orpheus for Narrator and Chamber Orchestra *
Overture: In Praise of Folly
Pageant and Proclamation *
Perimeters for Clarinet and Piano

Piano Sonata no. 1
Piano Sonata no. 2
Piano Sonata no. 3 *
Piano Sonata no. 4 *
Piano Sonata no. 5
Poem for Soprano and Chamber Ensemble *
Poeme for Violin and Orchestra *
Psalms for Chorus
A Red, Red Rose for Voice and Piano
Serenata for Chamber Orchestra *
Sinfonia no. 1
Sinfonia no. 2
Sinfonia no. 3 *
Sonata for Two Pianos
Sonata for Violin and Piano no. 1
Sonata for Violin and Piano no. 2 *
Spatials for Piano
Spektra for Piano
Spires for Organ *
String Quartet no. 1
String Quartet no. 2
Tangents for Chamber Orchestra *
Three Pieces for Organ
Two Pieces for Organ *
Variations for Orchestra
Windset for Woodwind Quintet *

---

* Commissioned works

Appendix C: Articles

The Audiophile Voice
    Comini, Kathleen. "Interview with Dr. George Walker." Vol. 7, no. 1.
Fanfare Magazine
    Burwasser, Peter. "Walker." July/August 1997.
HBCU College Algebra Reform Consortium
    Newsletter of the HBCU College Algebra Reform Consortium, Vignette—George Walker.
Library of Congress
    Walker, George. "Four Poems" (original).
    Walker, George. "The Lot of the Black Composer" (keynote address from UNISYS African-American Composers Forum, 1992).
New Music Connoisseur
    "George Walker: A Conversation with Bruce Duffie." March 9, 2001.
New York Times
    Blumenthal, Ralph. "A Pulitzer Winner's Overnight Success of 60 Years." April 11, 1996.
    Deitch, Joseph. "A Career Composing Classical Music." July 15, 1990.
    Finn, Terri Lowen. "A Serious Composer Talks about the Path to Success." New Jersey section, February 8, 1981.
    Plaskin, Glenn. "A Composer Who Backed into the Business." January 10, 1982.
    Walker, George. "Make Room for Black Classical Music." November 3, 1993.
    "A Wonderful Birthday Tribute," May 2003.

Philadelphia Inquirer
   Valdes, Leslie. "Yes, He's a Great Composer." October 31, 1996.
Scarecrow Press
   Belt, Lida M. "Interview with George Theophilus Walker." In *The Black Composer Speaks*, ed. David N. Baker, Lida M. Belt, and Herman C. Hudson, 1978.
Star-Ledger
   Adamo, Mark. "Looking Past the Prize." January 19, 1997.
   Redmond, Michael. "Music Community Says Pulitzer Long Overdue." April 14, 1996.
Stereophile
   Buckley, Dan. "The Music of George Walker." November 1997.
Washington Post
   McLellan, Joseph. "Hometown Homage to a D.C. Composer." June 8, 1997.

Appendix D: Reviews

ORCHESTRA

Address for Orchestra (1959)
"A major piece of great energy and thrust whose three movements are culminated by a moving Passacaglia." (*San Francisco Chronicle*)
"A powerful Passacaglia." (*New York Times*)
"The product of a craftsman whose compositional horizons are international, this is an evocation filled with strength and urgent communication—the metrical patterns constantly fluctuating and creating a rhythmic impression of linear propulsiveness, the sonorities strange and experimental, the harmonic language highly chromatic." (*Baltimore Sun*)

An Eastman Overture (1983)
"A tight-knit, brilliantly orchestrated and dramatic work" (*Washington Post*)

Folk Songs for Orchestra (1990)
"These moving transformations of simple melodic elements—encased like gems within Walker's sensitive, original, meditative settings—into far-ranging statements invite repeat listening." (Amazon.com)

Hoopla (A Touch of Glee) (2005)
"Energetic paean . . . strength and will combined with vibrancy and more than a bit of boldness." (*Las Vegas Review-Journal*)

Lyric for Strings (1946)
"Deserves to be as popular as the string elegies by Grieg, Faure and Elgar." (*Classical New Jersey*)

"Intense, haunting, lyrical beauty." (*News Journal*, Mansfield, Ohio)
"Hushed beauty and passionate intensity." (*American Record Guide*)
"A gorgeous find." (*Cincinnati Enquirer*)
"A finely crafted and deeply felt piece." (*Philadelphia Inquirer*)
"Intensely moving and beautiful." (*High Fidelity*)
"It reminds one of Barber's Adagio for Strings, only less sentimental and ultimately, more profound." (*Baltimore Evening Sun*)
"A Masterpiece!" (*Fanfare Magazine*)
"One of the most beautiful pieces ever written." (*News Journal*, Wilmington, Delaware)
"A gem." (*Baltimore Sun*)
"As a piece of gentle art . . . it has few peers." (*Philadelphia Inquirer*)

Pageant and Proclamation (1997)
"A statement of tremendous power." (*Classical New Jersey*)

Sinfonia no. 3 (2003)
"Rugged expressiveness . . . muscular, thrusting gestures . . . a dark prism of colors . . . a clangorous finale." (*Detroit Free Press*)
"Rugged expressiveness . . . expertly controlled sway of tension and release . . . dark prism of colors . . . an enthusiastic performance." (*Detroit News* and *Detroit Free Press*)

CONCERTOS

Concerto for Piano and Orchestra (1975)
"The blockbuster of the evening, full of poetry and pyrotechnics." (*Washington Star*)
"A mastery of serial effects with the more traditional values of dramatic statement, effective instrumental color, attractive melodic motion." (*Washington Post*)

Concerto for Trombone and Orchestra (1957)
"A bold virtuoso vehicle of considerable melodic and rhythmic power that speaks with a deeply personal voice." (*High Fidelity*)
"The finest work of its kind for trombone." (*The Music Connection*)

Dialogus for Cello and Orchestra (1976)
"A technically brilliant showcase for a virtuoso cellist." (*Cleveland Plain Dealer*)

Poeme for Violin and Chamber Orchestra (1991)

"An elegantly crafted piece by a distinguished composer." (*St. Paul Pioneer Press*)

"Dramatically expressive, lyrically intense." (Record International Catalogue)

CHAMBER ORCHESTRA

Tangents (1999)

"A work of originality and power." (Records International Catalogue)

"Powerful, weighty stuff." (*Music and Vision*)

Orpheus (1994)

"Vividly colored (especially dramatic use of the brass) . . . filled with jagged flashes of emotion." (Record International Catalogue)

Folk Songs for Orchestra (1990)

"A tone-poem-like transformation of simple melodic elements into an expressively far-ranging statement." (*Washington Post*)

Serenata for Chamber Orchestra (1983)

"A work of challenging sonorities in three subtly contrasted movements . . . a strong spirit commemorated with dignity, distance, and power." (*Detroit Monitor*)

CHAMBER MUSIC

Abu (2004)

"Powerful . . . wondrously luminous." (*Philadelphia Inquirer*)

Poeme for Soprano and Chamber Ensemble (1987)

"A masterpiece of musical blend . . . a devastating work, deserving of greater attention." (*Schenectady Gazette*)

Sonata for Violin and Piano no. 1 (1958)

"Powerful authenticity and dramatic expression . . . truly great music." (*Classical New Jersey*)

"It's astonishing to this listener that Walker's Violin Sonata No. 1 has yet to become a staple for recitalists. . . . This is beautiful, deeply moving music, straight from the heart, and its appeal to the most traditional of audiences is virtually guaranteed." (*Star-Ledger*, Newark, New Jersey)

Violin and Piano Sonata no. 2 (1979)

"Walker's Violin Sonata is a knockout." (*Tucson Citizen*)

String Quartet no. 2 (1968)

"The writing is delicate, clear-textured and fluid, sensitive to the need for dramatic phrases as contrast and highlight. For all its transparency, the music has admirable momentum, fostered less by strong rhythms than by the constant variation in instrumental color." (*New York Times*)

PIANO MUSIC

Prelude and Caprice (1945, 1941)

"Prelude and Caprice. . . . Superb craftsmanship." (*Classics Today*)

Guido's Hand (1986)

"A remarkably eloquent piece." (*Star-Ledger*, Newark, New Jersey)

Sonata for Piano no. 1 (1953)

"A Major work . . . comparable to Barber's Sonata." (*Fanfare Magazine*)

"In a word, masterly." (*New York Times*)

Sonata for Piano no. 2 (1956)

"Powerful, idiomatic piano writing." (*Buffalo News*)

"An acknowledged masterpiece." (Barnes and Noble.com)

Sonata for Piano no. 4 (1984)

"A distinctive work of American modernism—complex, yet immediately appealing, built, for the most part, on the contrast between stark proclamations and more lyrical passages, leading to a rousing toccata." (*New York Times*)

Sonata for Two Pianos (1975)

"This terse sonata was notable for its inventive fantasy and magical piano writing. . . . Here is a most effective addition to the piano repertory which should be heard again and often. Terrific piece!" (*San Francisco Chronicle*)

"This composition is bristling with ideas, motoric energy, sophisti-cated craftsmanship and, in the adagio, incandescent beauty" (*The Jewish Week*, New York)

VOCAL MUSIC

Cantata for Soprano, Tenor, Organ, Boys Choir and Chamber Orchestra (1982)
 "This is a haunting, inventive piece . . . thought-provoking yet ac-cessible." (*Fanfare Magazine*)
Lilacs for Voice and Orchestra (1995)
 "Melodies soar above the orchestra like the star and bird symbols in the text." (*Detroit Free Press*)
 "A poignant and dramatic work with a strongly lyrical vocal line and strikingly original orchestration." (Records International Catalogue)
 "A dense, dark work that penetrates deeply into the soul of Whit-man's response to the assassination of a great leader." (*Atlanta Constitution*)
 "There is wonderful music in this cycle, which is profoundly re-sponsive to the images of the text—you can hear the sway of lilacs in the rhythm, smell their fragrance in the harmony." (*Boston Globe*)
 "A style of great emotional expressivity. . . . The masterful text-setting is accompanied by imaginative, evocative orchestral writing." (Barnes and Noble.com)
 "A work of great surface beauty and immediacy of appeal. The vocal line soars and spirals in melismas of ardent grief; the music captures the sway and fragrance of lilacs as well as the freedom of a bird's flight." (*Boston Globe*)
 "Masterpiece." (*The Audiophile Voice*)
Mass for Soloists, Chorus, Organ, and Orchestra (1977)
 "A powerful and poignant re-interpretation of the liturgical mean-ing of the ancient Latin text." (*Baltimore Evening Sun*)
Songs
 "Walker's way with Emily Dickinson is distinctly personal and powerful." (*American Record Guide*)

"The songs are as outstanding as they are varied." (*Fanfare Magazine*)

"Intriguing, sometimes daring melodies." (*Houston Chronicle*)

MISCELLANEOUS COMMENTS

"George Walker is one of the most highly regarded and successful composers of the late twentieth century." (*Musical Quarterly*, Fall 2000)

"A great composer who's been at his job for over fifty years." (*Positive Feedback*, 2006)

"His acknowledged masterpiece is for solo piano, the Sonata no. 2." (Yahoo! Biography, 2000)

"Walker has made an important and rewarding contribution to the piano repertoire. . . . Music of originality without artificiality, born of his imagination and his search for precise expression." (*Piano and Keyboard Magazine*, 1997)

Index

About the Author

George Walker was born in Washington, DC, in 1922. He began the study of piano when he was five years old. After graduating from high school at age fourteen, he received a scholarship to Oberlin College. Finishing at the top of his conservatory class four years later, Mr. Walker was admitted to the Curtis Institute of Music, where he studied piano with Rudolf Serkin and composition with Rosario Scalero.

He was presented in a Town Hall debut recital by Mr. and Mrs. Efrem Zimbalist in 1945, the first black concert pianist to appear in that hall. After a phenomenal success in New York, Mr. Walker also became the first black pianist to play with the Philadelphia Orchestra, performing in the Third Piano Concerto of Rachmaninoff with Eugene Ormandy conducting.

There were additional firsts: in 1950 Mr. Walker was signed by a major management company, National Concert Artists; in 1953 he made an unprecedented tour of seven European countries; and in 1956 he became the first black recipient of the doctor of musical arts degree from the Eastman School of Music.

George Walker has taught at Dillard University; the Dalcroze School of Music; the New School for Social Research; the University of Colorado; Rutgers University, where he was chairman of the Music Department; the Peabody Institute of Johns Hopkins University; and the University of Delaware, where he held the first minority chair.

He has been the recipient of many awards, including a Fulbright Fellowship, two Rockefeller Fellowships, a John Hay Whitney Fellowship, two Guggenheim Fellowships, and six honorary doctoral degrees. In 1996 he became the first black composer to receive the Pulitzer Prize in Music and was inducted into the American Classical Music Hall of Fame in 2000.